Lost in the Middle?

Lost in the Middle?

Claiming an inclusive faith
for moderate Christians who are
both liberal and evangelical

WESLEY J. WILDMAN

STEPHEN CHAPIN GARNER

THE
ALBAN
INSTITUTE

Herndon, Virginia
www.alban.org

The Alban Institute
2121 Cooperative Way, Suite 100
Herndon, VA 20171

Scripture quotations, are from the New Revised Standard Version of the Bible, © 1989, Division of Christian Education of the National Council of Churches of Christ in the United States of America, and are used by permission.

Cover design by Spark Design, LLC.

Library of Congress Cataloging-in-Publication Data

Wildman, Wesley J., 1961–
  Lost in the middle? : claiming an inclusive faith for Christians who are both liberal and evangelical / Wesley J. Wildman, Stephen Chapin Garner.
      p. cm.
  Includes bibliographical references.
  ISBN 978-1-56699-372-2
  1. Liberalism (Religion)—Protestant churches. 2. Evangelicalism. 3. Liberalism (Religion)—United States. 4. Evangelicalism—United States. I. Garner, Stephen Chapin, 1969–
II. Title.

  BR1615.W56 2009
  277.3'083—dc22
                                    2008053167

  09   10   11   12   13   VG   5   4   3   2   1

For Suzanne

For Tammie

Contents

Preface

We write this book for Christians who feel theologically and spiritually displaced. There are plenty of them. They feel lost in the middle between the noisy extremes of religion and politics and long to feel right at home right where they are. They sense that it is possible to ignore the oversimplifications of left and right and, instead, move deeper into their faith. But they are not quite sure how to do that. They know the path they seek has something to do with love because they understand the power of love to unite people of different kinds, to overcome alienation, and to bring about transforming forgiveness. If only they could understand their situation clearly, perhaps they could plot the path ahead.

This book speaks directly to such Christians. It is a guidebook to help them learn how to describe their moderate location in a positive and compelling way. It will stretch and educate, and it needs to do that, because this is not one of those problems with an obvious "silver bullet" answer. But for the person who identifies with the sketch in the opening chapter, this is probably the book for which you have been waiting.

It is easy to understand the pain of displacement, of feeling lost amid everyone else's certainties. Christians are often lumped in coarse ideological categories that don't mesh with the texture of an individual's or a church's faith convictions. Protestant Christians and churches are generally sorted into four stereotypes: liberal, evangelical, conservative, and fundamentalist. People of faith are, by and large, aware of these categories. Fundamentalists typically insist the Bible is the inerrant and historically accurate word of God. Conservative Christians tend to have an intense interest seeing their faith-based morality formed into legislative action. Evangelical Christians appear to be all about loving, serving, and having a personal relationship with Jesus. Liberal Christians frequently focus on issues of social justice and inclusion.

So, if you believe God literally created the world in six days, you must be a fundamentalist. If you want to take your local school system to court in hopes of having science teachers add creationism to their curriculum, you must be a conservative Christian. If you believe Adam and Eve were created so Jesus would need to be born into the world, you must be an evangelical Christian. If you believe Adam and Steve have as much right to be married as Adam and Eve, you must be a liberal Christian.

People rarely look just like their caricatures. There are liberal Christians who love Jesus. There are evangelical Christians who care about protecting the environment. There are conservative Christians who embrace their gay sons and daughters. There are fundamentalist Christians who have no interest in reviving the biblical practice of having men and women stoned on the town square for adultery.

Overlaps and tensions between these labels further complicate matters. Some fundamentalist and conservative Christians would claim the evangelical label, and some liberals wish they could. Yet there are plenty of evangelical Christians who would consider themselves neither conservative nor fundamentalist. Liberalism is similarly diverse, and the divisions are almost as pointed. Liberal Christians tend to be wary of evangelical, conservative, and fundamentalist Christians alike, and that feeling is reciprocated. Likewise, many Christians are suspicious of fundamentalists, and that suspicion is returned in spades.

In short, we have created a mess where Protestant Christians of all persuasions are at odds with each other. Perhaps we should not be surprised when these faith categories are often used carelessly or contemptuously. Humans are social and territorial beings who need to feel their world makes sense and their values are reflected in the patterns of social life. We readily fight for what we believe, and we defend our moral and religious territory with as much vigor as we protect our physical space. These are the undertows beneath the tides of contemporary as well as ancient culture wars, and the wellspring of divisive religious categories.

One side benefit of infighting among Protestants is that their traditional suspicion of Roman Catholics has abated somewhat. Not many decades ago, a Protestant marrying a Catholic was often a difficulty of Romeo-and-Juliet proportions for both families. That's not as common these days. But there is a balancing disadvantage. In our era, a religious conservative marrying a religious liberal may be even more difficult for some families to accept. And that scenario can happen within the Jewish and Muslim faiths as easily as within Christianity.

Meanwhile, countless Catholics are deeply disillusioned with the Mother Church's patriarchal authoritarianism, with its condescending attitude toward women, and with its sometimes shockingly protective approach to the perversity of sexual abuse of children and young adults by Catholic priests. In despair, many of them have migrated to Protestant churches in search of another spiritual home, while other Catholics forsake Christian worship altogether. The resentment is fierce among both those who leave and those who stay.

Sadly, these patterns of hostility are becoming increasingly obvious. Within Protestantism, the quiet majority is stirring uneasily. They recognize the liberal or evangelical labels don't apply neatly to them. They know from long experience that noisy, anxious people magnify rather than solve problems, often rushing past simpler, calmer solutions on their way to name-calling and inflammatory behavior. They believe the church should model for the world a kind of community that rises above territorial instincts and insults, one that stresses love and acceptance more than social identity and security.

This quiet majority includes uneasy evangelicals, troubled liberals, uncomfortable conservatives, and disillusioned Catholics—but probably not fundamentalists or extreme liberals. These folk feel confused by what is happening and want guidance. They want to know whether it is possible to be a Christian with both liberal and evangelical instincts. They long to feel at home rather than lost in the middle.

Do you long for a Christian faith that takes the Bible seriously while recognizing that God has yet more light to shed on the world? Do you desire a Christian faith that can proclaim Jesus Christ unapologetically while embracing the diversity and mystery of God's creation? Do you ache for a Christian faith that is passionate and personal while at the same time intellectually robust, gracefully generous, and globally sensitive? Those are the longings of a liberal and evangelical Christian faith. Those are desires we address in this book and seek to cultivate in our lives and work and in local churches.

We are convinced that discerning Christians and churches can choose to transcend the liberal versus evangelical conflict. We also contend that for the Christian church to be authentic, vibrant, and socially relevant in the future, individual people of faith, and the institutions that nurture their faith, must find ways to celebrate and practice the highest virtues of both liberal and evangelical Christianity. Our efforts are intended to help pastors, pastoral leaders, seminarians, and thoughtful Christians unite the compassionate openness and social activism of liberal Christianity with the corporate magnetism and spiritual fervor of evangelical Christianity.

That longed-for unity is far from easy or obvious. It requires patient work grounded in reliable knowledge and inspired by confidence in the power of love. To that end, we have tried to observe how the liberal-evangelical church manages diversity. We have endeavored to comprehend the principles guiding its decisions and the narratives structuring its identity. We have pondered why some Christians feel strongly called to embrace its corporate life as their context for Christian growth and discipleship. We have also made an effort to grasp why some people find this kind of church unattractive or a betrayal of Christian truth. Not everyone *wants* to find unity among Christians of different stripes, especially across the liberal versus evangelical divide. But it is important to see that such unity is *possible* for those who choose it, especially when they have the right kind of support. For discerning moderate Christians, this feels like a better way and a higher calling.

⌐⟍

We have been tempted to leave behind all of these labels and strike out in a new direction, simply laying out a satisfying and challenging vision of Christian faith and church. We have also been tempted to follow the trend of inventing new labels, trying them on to see if they fit. If conservatives can be compassionate and liberals progressive, then maybe simultaneously liberal and evangelical Christians can be "Progressives for Jesus" or "Radically Inclusive Bible Believers." Or maybe not! We have resisted these temptations, despite urging from some readers, especially out of loyalty to our imagined audience. The silent majority needs help where they are, in the terms that they know. To them, new labels merely repackage a problem. Truth in advertising should be paramount.

In fact, we think the words "liberal" and "evangelical" are quite poorly understood. Both are wonderful words with impressive heritages. Understanding them well makes it easier to see how they fit together naturally, how they both can be important features of a vibrant faith and a radically inclusive church community. We know these labels can become caricatures, so we use them advisedly. But they are ingrained in contemporary Christian life, and we need them to express the richness of a profoundly traditional vision of Christian faith and church life.

Of course, we have met extreme liberals and rigorous evangelicals who are convinced that trying to nurture a moderate identity for liberal-evangelical Christian faith and church life amounts to a sellout. They say moderates are simply muddled and should pick a side and fight for its vital principles rather than seeking to transcend the conflict. But these advice givers don't grasp the situation of moderates.

Moderates might feel lost in the middle, but *they are not confused about what they believe.* If forced to pick a side, which side should moderates pick? Moderates are uncomfortable in either wing of the polarized religious environment. They appreciate principles and practices on both sides of the liberal versus evangelical divide. They are frustrated by the conflict and eager for a principled way of speaking about the moderate, inclusive, passionate kind of Christians they have become and are becoming. Moderates are quite capable of fighting for what they believe. But we think the fight moderates are invited to join by extreme proponents of both sides is the wrong fight.

The more important battle for moderate Christians is with a society that lives far beneath the radically inclusive message of Jesus Christ. This battle is also, gently but definitely, with Christians who are so attached to fighting each other or so comfortable with strangled decay or blind togetherness that they have forgotten how radical, how challenging, how joyful the Christian gospel really is. Moderate Christians of the liberal-evangelical type may have been formed as liberals or evangelicals, mainliners or independents, fundamentalists or Pentecostals. But they have migrated to where they are now in search of something else, something more difficult and more rewarding.

This position does not reflect any lack of faith or conviction, despite the criticisms of the extremes. Rather, moderate Christians find distasteful the reduction of theology and morality and politics to black-and-white contrasts. They are difficult to budge because they sense that their moderate ways are wise. But they know firsthand that it is not easy being true to their moral and religious instincts, or even identifying them, when prevailing social conflict means that the loudest voices always articulate somebody else's views.

Understandably, most people struggle to express their reasons for rejecting the extremes of Christian theology and political ideology. Many of them do not even have a label for what they are and seek to become. Yet they speak movingly about their intuitive reactions, negative and positive; to their political and cultural environment; and to the churches they have visited and to which they have belonged. Perhaps this mix of graceful speech and inarticulateness is to be expected of moderate Christians trying to construct a progressive, inclusive, passionate, Christ-centered faith identity. They have to react to what is already well defined around them. To us, this everyday fumbling for words is an invitation to present a way of thinking about Christianity that may help seminary students, pastors, and lay church leaders with both liberal and evangelical instincts become more eloquent about their own commitments.

This is not a book you will read in one sitting. It is a guide-book for people with a purpose in mind when they read it. It will make you think and stretch you in new directions. But it does deliver what we promise. For those who feel lost in the middle but feel sure they are in the right place anyway, this book offers a way of understanding their situation, their heritage, and their choices. It will help them learn how to claim their liberal and evangelical instincts with articulate confidence.

In closing these prefatory remarks, it may help our readers to know more about us, particularly because the act of commend-ing a vision of Christian faith and life is such a personal one, for us and for our readers alike.

We are both liberals and both evangelicals—though we know liberals and evangelicals who would deny us these labels in their senses of them. Both of us are white men, husbands and fathers, pastors and preachers, and lifelong learners. We are friends and collaborators. But we are quite dissimilar in some ways. One of us is more conservative in Christian doctrinal matters, while the other is more conservative in moral convictions. Our spirituali-ties are quite different. One of us is a thinker and the other a doer. One of us is a homegrown American, while the other is an immigrant. One of us can play table tennis, and the other merely thinks he can. And that brings up another similarity: we are fond of expressing affection through gentle teasing.

If our dissimilarities mimic some of the diversity in contem-porary American Christianity, then our shared feelings and com-mon views, as well as our friendship, express the possibilities inherent in putting liberal and evangelical back together, which is where we think they once were, where they sometimes still are, and where they always properly belong.

Acknowledgments

We have not considered these matters in isolation. On the contrary, we have experimented in congregations and seminary classrooms; we have organized discussions with ministerial colleagues and lay Christian leaders, with sociologists, historians, and theologians; and we have distilled conclusions from the mix of thoughtful comments and visceral reactions we have had the privilege of hearing.

A meeting of Christ Clarion Fellowship served as a test readership for parts of the book. This is an extraordinary group of young Christian pastors with both liberal and evangelical instincts, smart as whips and with energy to burn. They give us hope for the future of the church. We learned a lot from that weekend experience and thank Andrew Warner, Eric Dupee, Jennifer Thomas, Kate Murphy, Laura Everett, Nicole Yonkman, Steve Lewis, Bill Lamar, and Van Moody.

Another test audience was a seminary class at Boston University that read a draft of the manuscript and discussed it with the authors. We received helpful feedback and lots of encouragement from eleven eager, talented, and diverse masters' students: Wesley Alves, John Brink, Jennifer Douglas, Jongwook Hong, Hyun Woo Lee, Jaemin Lee, Jim Pittman, Carol Raymond, Drew Tennant, Kathy Waters, and Kate Wilkinson.

Several pastors and scholars have sent us comments or engaged us in conversation. Neither of us is trained as an academic historian, so we particularly appreciate the comments of David Hempton and Dana Robert; the remaining peculiarities in the historical material are fully our responsibility. We prized the comments and thoughts of Nancy Ammerman, Kristy Besada, Delwin Brown, Rodney Clapp, Brandon Daniel-Hughes, Joanna Hill, Chad Johns, Vaughan McTernan, Hank Pietersee, Tony Robinson, Bryan Stone, and Suzanne Woolston Bossert. And then there are the many dozens, surely hundreds, of conversations about one or another aspect of the book in a host of diverse contexts with an unendingly colorful array of fascinating people.

This book is full of true stories, and only true stories, modified to maintain confidentiality. These stories drive home the personal quality of the quest for a faith that refuses false comfort for the sake of authentically inclusive love. We hope the readers who think they recognize themselves in these stories will understand the roles they have played in forming our thinking and enjoy their anonymous appearance in this book. We owe a debt of gratitude to them, as well as to the many pastors, teachers, colleagues, and saints who have helped in the formation of our own Christian faith over the years.

We are grateful to our publisher Richard Bass for publishing an article on the theme of the book in the Alban Institute's *Congregations* magazine, and to Del Brown for republishing that article on the progressivechristianwitness.com website. We are particularly thankful to Richard for his confidence in the project and his willingness to bring this book to a wider audience, as well as the companion volume, *Found in the Middle!* We are fortunate indeed to have Virginia Amos as our editor. A sensitive and intelligent person, Virginia displayed sympathy for our task of conveying complex ideas to a mixed audience and offered excellent advice.

The website LiberalEvangelical.org aims to empower radically moderate Christians and to offer resources for creatively inclusive congregations. That website contains study guides for this book and for its companion volume, *Found in the Middle!*, as well as a host of other useful resources. We are delighted to acknowledge the Center for Practical Theology at Boston University School of Theology for a faculty research grant that helped to support the construction of the site.

The "primal communities" that formed our thinking for this book are ordinary Christians in the two settings most familiar to us: congregations and seminaries. This is where we have done most of our learning about how frustrated, neglected, marginalized, and lost many moderate Christians feel; how strongly they long to feel at home in the middle; and how profoundly they believe in the power of love to unite people across some degree of ideological and theological difference. We have been deeply impressed by their instinctive confidence that there must be a way even when they could not find it. The way we describe in this book may not be the longed-for answer that some of them seek, but it will be that for many.

We are indebted to our life partners, Suzanne and Tammie. Their support and devotion is more perfect than mere mortals have any right to expect. We hope they appreciate this book as speaking to their own souls, even as it springs from ours under their shaping influence.

PART I

Haunting Questions and One-Sided Answers

CHAPTER 1

Five Haunting Questions

Religious messages from the left and right reach into the lives of moderate Christians, whether invited or not, offering answers to potent existential questions. The result is a confusing labyrinth of contradictory spiritual and theological advice. The child in church school, the teenager approaching confirmation, the seminary student, the mature believer, and the religious seeker all grapple with these questions and often experience dissatisfaction with the standard answers pressed upon them.

An older church member in a former congregation told one of us that he had figured out how to handle his faith questions. Instead of seeking answers to his actual questions, he simply adjusts what he hears in sermons and studies to suit his own perspective. Like an editor of his own private magazine, he collects ideas from everywhere, disposing of some while keeping others, usually in a modified form that suits his evolving faith. But he also confessed that this often amounts to training himself to keep quiet about his faith and his doubts for the sake of belonging to a group he treasures. He'd love to talk about his faith, but he can't do that without making waves so he stays quiet.

The problem of open discussion of faith issues is even more obvious with young people. From our own experience as youth workers, we know how this lack of frankness about difficult questions makes church and faith an awkward proposition for young people. For them, one-sided answers to the haunting questions of life cause obvious pain and confusion. It is heartbreaking to watch and genuinely difficult to know how to help.

If these questions were merely conceptual in character, then the problem would not be so difficult. Most people would handle diversity of faith advice by ignoring what doesn't interest them and investing in their local spiritual homes. The intellectual types for whom this practical approach falls short would read widely and study to gain the understanding they seek. It would be like mathematics—interested people study the problems of mathematics, but most people only use what they need and forget the rest. The problem with religious diversity and polarization is that the questions we ask are deeply personal. The answers matter profoundly to us on many levels. Much of what we hear out there just rubs us the wrong way. Only a fortunate few discover answers that ring deeply true.

Moderates might be a large group in contemporary Christianity, but they are underrepresented as far as theological support and spiritual guidance are concerned. The extremes get their questions answered, even if they don't always feel convinced by the answers they receive. But the personal translation of theological polarization is confusion and quiet desperation for those in the middle, all politely covered over as if moderate Christians are not entitled to expect anyone to address their serious questions directly. Moderate Christianity is, in many places, like a spiritual desert, short of nourishing food and life-giving water. This is true even in seminaries, where students have so much to learn, often amid emotional and spiritual stress, that they cannot really deal with their spiritual needs—a fact that may surprise some church people who believe that seminary students are blessed with unshakable confidence. It is also true in church communities, where communal support for existentially loaded faith questions is sometimes more coercive than empathetic and other times just absent.

Moderate Christians should not have to stay quiet about their faith amid the sometimes artificial clarities of left and right. They deserve intellectually persuasive and spiritually compelling answers. The good news is that the answers exist. But moderates have to contend with profoundly different visions of faith in order to learn how to grasp those answers for themselves. In each case, *those answers are not bumper-sticker slogans but syntheses of thought and action that call for lifestyles of radical discipleship, devoted study, and compassionate social engagement.* That is a theme we will return to several times in the course of this book.

We will discuss five key existential questions that trouble moderate Christians. We could broach many other questions here, but we focus on five that we think recur among moderate Christians with liberal and evangelical instincts. We present these questions by means of stories based, as always in this book, on actual people and events.

PLURALISM AND RELATIVISM: ARE WE RIGHT?

Jack and his wife and three children attend church every Sunday they are in town. Church is simply part of who Jack is and has been since he was a child. He likes his church. He enjoys how his pastor can take the Bible and relate it to everyday life, but Jack squirms in his seat every time his pastor says that "Islam is of the devil and will be defeated." Jack's neighbor is a Muslim—a man of prayer, a faithful husband, a loving father, and a good neighbor. Jack is a committed Christian, but he can't bring himself to believe that his neighbor is going to go to hell because he attends a mosque and not a Christian church. He has tried talking about this to people he respects. At work, one of Jack's colleagues says, "All religions are the same—they make exclusive claims, which cancel each other out, so none of them can be believed." Jack's sister tells him, "It doesn't matter what religious path you choose so long as you choose one sincerely and stick to it faithfully." But Jack can't accept these variations on relativism either, because they don't do justice to his profound sense of relationship to God. Jack is stranded between clear answers that he can't believe wholeheartedly. He does not know how to trust his instincts, and he can't find anyone to guide him to a better place.

We hear Jack's question echoed by every thoughtful confirmation student, regardless of whether he or she decides to be confirmed: How do we know we are right? What about the Buddhists, the Hindus, and the Jews? Are they wrong? How can we be sure? The simple fact that so many Christians and Christian groups claim a unique and unquestionable understanding of divine truth can make even the most committed Christians scratch their heads. With so many different claims of truth out there, who is right? Is anyone right? Is it even possible to be right?

Lucinda is a member of a congregation that confirms children when they enter high school. Her son has to decide if he is going to be confirmed. These are the questions he puts to her when he arrives home after confirmation classes. Before scheduling a private meeting for her son with their pastor she tries her best to share her own beliefs. She tells her son that she has always been a Christian. Being a Christian "works" for her. She lets him know that she believes that God loves all people, even though their pastor insists that you have to accept Jesus Christ in your life to be saved. Lucinda's son takes all this in stride, but it doesn't help much. He quietly wonders why anyone would bother trying to be a Christian when Christians disagree so strongly on such basic issues. It seems to him that you have to become a fanatic to overcome natural uncertainty; only fanatics can shut down such simple but tough questions. Privately, Lucinda wonders if it is indeed possible to be a Christian if you don't believe everything you hear in church, if you don't trust your pastor's theological wisdom.

These questions can be deal breakers for a young person's decision to embrace the Christian way. But they bother mature Christians, too. If the Bible says Jesus is the only way, what will happen to Jews and Muslims, Hindus and Buddhists? If I'm not sure about the accuracy of certain stories in the Bible, how can I be certain of anything in the Bible? People need poised answers to these questions if they are to develop a deep and abiding religious commitment.

Most conservative Christians claim Jesus is the only way to a relationship with God. This strikes liberals as bluster, just barely covering an ocean of insecurity, usually accompanied by a lack of extended personal exposure to the admirable people of other religions whose spiritual standing conservative Christians so casually dismiss. Meanwhile, most liberal Christians are willing to affirm anything that works for a given individual. But this strikes conservatives as an ill-conceived flourish of generosity that amounts to an anti-advertisement for what is distinctively valuable in Christianity.

Neither of these approaches helps to address how we should deal with the diversity of religious claims and religious people in a way that honors the distinctiveness of Christian faith. Can we honor the faith traditions of others, like Jesus did when he extended his healing ministry to those beyond his Jewish faith, or are we supposed to make disciples of all people and all nations, like the early church often claimed? What should our response be when the Southern Baptist Convention proclaims that Christians should try to convert their Jewish friends and neighbors when we like our neighbors just the way they are?

Brushing these questions aside, pointing to the Bible and saying "it's all clearly written in there," answering every question with "it's a mystery," or telling people it is simply best to live with the questions because we don't have any answers—these approaches are no longer working, and they are a detriment to the church. With these sorts of answers to go on, Christians like Jack and Lucinda and her son become increasingly confused and frustrated. At some deep level they know there has to be a better way, but it is not one that they have ever heard about. In the meantime, while the search for genuine insight continues, their faith feels short on authenticity and wisdom, and they get tired of patiently waiting for understanding that never arrives.

PASSION AND POLITICS:
IF I LOVE JESUS, AM I A FREAK?

Mary and John have been looking for a church on and off for months. They have moved to the Midwest from the Northeast, though both of them grew up in the South. Mary is an orthopedic surgeon, and John is a high school English teacher. They have raised their two daughters, now approaching their teenage years, in the Christian church. Their faith is very important to Mary and John, but they prefer to practice it quietly, behind the scenes, with a fair degree of humility. As they church shopped they found only two kinds of churches. One sort of church is small and friendly, but you could go through an entire service without hearing anything significant about Jesus. Mary and John leave those services asking themselves how you can be a Christian without being in relationship with Jesus. The other kind of church is more campuslike, offering every program imaginable. The name of Jesus seems to be invoked in every other spoken word to the point of tedium, much like the never-ending praise songs that are projected on the walls and sung until the congregation is either spirit-filled or stir-crazy. Mary and John want to attend a church that focuses its life on Jesus Christ, but they don't want to have to look and act like fanatics either. What are they to do?

This is a problem for Mary and John and many other moderate Christians. If I love Jesus, do I have to become a fanatic? Do I need to wear a "What Would Jesus Do?" bracelet everywhere I go, or one of those T-shirts that says "got jesus?" instead of "got milk?" Am I going to be lumped together in the minds of my peers with televangelists such as Jerry Falwell and Pat Robertson? If Jesus is the essential ingredient in the Christian life and the Christian church, how do I include him in my life without looking like a bigot or an idiot? It is the fear of many thoughtful Christians: On the street corner and on television, the people that most noisily profess love and devotion to Jesus are people they don't find attractive and do not want to emulate. These people make following Jesus seem repulsive or offensive.

Perhaps the answer is simply to drop Jesus out of the equation altogether, as most Unitarian churches have done, or minimize Jesus talk, as many mainline churches do. Perhaps there is a thinking person's church out there where someone can be vaguely "spiritual" and not judgmental. But this will never be an option for Mary and John. They have found purpose for life and personal transformation through their relationship with Jesus Christ. They will not give him up because their Christian experience makes no sense without him at the center of it. In fact, they would gladly invite unchurched neighbors to their community of faith if they could just find one that seemed to meet them where they are. Mary and John want to be faithful disciples of Christ, and they want their children to possess similar faith convictions. They want their Christian beliefs to inform decisions they make at work, at home, and in their community. They just don't want to have to practice their faith with a "Honk if you love Jesus" bumper sticker on their car.

Belief and Doubt: Am I Making This Up?

Liberal, conservative, or somewhere in between, there is a subtle question that often wafts through our minds when night falls and we are left alone with only our thoughts to distract us. Is this real? Is this faith I profess to believe just a crutch? Is my faith experience just a projection of my emotional needs and my hopes for the future? Is my idea of God just a transference reaction to unresolved issues with my parents? Which do I find more compelling, the gospels of Matthew, Mark, Luke, and John or the theories of Feuerbach, Marx, Nietzsche, and Freud?

These questions afflict Janice from time to time. She finds that critical reflection on her religious beliefs usually produces more questions than answers. It reminds her of college, where she experienced the odd phenomenon that the more she learned, the less sure she became of the knowledge she had. In deep thought, the idea of God she inherited comes to seem suddenly implausible and suspiciously convenient, as if customized to suit her emotional needs. Reflecting on the unfathomable divine nature leads her to wonder whether perhaps her faith is just an escape from the harsh realities of the world. Perhaps humanity has invented concepts such as God, heaven, hell, and the resurrection as a shield against the painful prospect that human life is a cosmic accident lived under the threat of annihilation with no more meaning beyond the flowing patterns of energy and matter that hold her fragile frame together.

In such a state of questioning reverie, Janice struggles to remember those sacred experiences, those holy awakening moments when she felt the hand of God powerfully in her life. Those are the moments she swore she would never forget. But now she can't remember why they were so compelling, so unquestionable. Her faint memory of them cannot sustain her against the dismaying questions that assail her faith. And what she can remember of them doesn't seem to count for much when she considers the capacity of the human psyche to create comfort and the power of human groups to conjure worlds of meaning, whether or not they are true.

Janice has turned to the church, and to other religious experts, for answers. She wants someone to take her questions seriously while offering her a path to follow that will allow for some insight into the truth that she senses abides deeply within her own skeptical feelings. Unfortunately, most evangelical Christians seem so firm in their faith convictions that she wonders if they have ever harbored any doubts like hers. Liberal Christians, on the other hand, seem to resist concrete beliefs like the plague, as if answers can only kill faith, and that leaves her frustrated.

Feeling lost and uncertain, Janice remembers Rev. Eaton praying in her living room the night her grandfather died. She wondered how anyone could pray so beautifully and effortlessly. She saw in Rev. Eaton a true man of God—but now she wonders whether she was just making that up at a time of profound grief. She thinks of the saints of the church who gave their lives for what they believed—but were they fanatics? She ponders the miracle of the church itself; how it started in relative obscurity on the shores of Galilee and now makes its home in that brick building in the center of her town and thousands of other towns—but is faith merely institutional momentum? She reads Paul's letters and thinks she sees there a life lived with the passion and conviction of faith—but was he psychologically unbalanced?

Finally, she sets aside the internal debate, telling herself that "faith is the assurance of things hoped for, the conviction of things not seen" (Hebrews 11:1) and that fears and faith must go hand in hand. Her hope and experience get the better of her and she finds that she tries to convince herself that "there is no way I made this all up." And, for the time being, she leaves it at that, uneasily hoping that one day she will find someone, or some church, or some way of understanding her faith that can shed light on her doubts without turning everything into the crisp black-and-white contrasts that always leave her feeling on the wrong side of someone else's idea of faith.

RELIGION AND SCIENCE: HOW DO I RECONCILE CONFLICTING PICTURES OF REALITY?

Dave hunts for fossils with his five-year-old son Sam on a shale beach on one of the Finger Lakes in New York. Even at age five, Dave's son has a well-developed sense of faith. Sam loves to talk about God, Jesus, and Bible stories. Sam always welcomes the opportunity to offer blessings at mealtimes, and he will sometimes suggest that the family pray before a long car trip or before a significant event. Sam also loves looking for beach glass and fossils. Sam found his first fossil this year; Dave embellished a bit and told Sam it was the best fossil he had ever seen. "How old is it, Dad?" "Millions of years old I suspect." "Were these fossils here when the dinosaurs were here?" "I guess." "God made the dinosaurs, right?" "Yes, Sam." "Are there dinosaur stories in the Bible?" "I don't think so." "Why not?"

At five years of age, Sam might be pining for a good story about Abraham and dinosaurs. But Dave gets to thinking about how different the world pictures of the Bible and modern science are. Like many Christians, Dave finds himself stuck between the revealed truths of faith and the discoveries and theories of scientific reason. In another few years, Sam is going to ask him how that fossil fits with the Bible's stories about the creation of the world. How will Dave answer his son then? What answer can he offer that will help Sam understand the complexities of the world while still developing his son's genuinely beautiful passion for faith? Dave knows some Christians simply dismiss scientific knowledge that doesn't seem to be supported by biblical witness, but to him that is simpleminded and shortsighted. And yet he doesn't want to tell his son the Bible is just a collection of important moral teachings because Dave doesn't believe that himself. He believes the Bible contains the truth of God; he's just not sure how to put it all together.

Dave's questions challenge all of us. What happens when the Bible appears to be wrong? How does a Christian respond when science seems to swat away every claim of truth the Bible has to offer? The world was created in six days, and God took a break on the seventh. This claim seems to fall into the same category as the belief that the Earth is flat and that our little whirling globe is the center of the universe. The scientific interpretation of the fossil record alone contradicts six-day creationism. Add Darwin to the mix, and from its very first chapters the Bible appears to be an ancient repository of scientifically primitive myths. Six days! How could anyone ever believe that in our age? And if you can't believe that, what about the virgin birth, the sun standing still for Joshua, Noah's flood, Jonah and the great fish ferry, Jesus walking on water, and the Easter claim that Jesus Christ rose from the dead?

A self-avowed conservative Christian evangelist was a guest in a college religion class at Northeastern University. He talked about his faith. He talked about the truth of the Bible. He talked about the inerrancy of scripture. One of the students in the class asked about some of the inconsistencies in the Bible. Why do the four gospels depict Jesus in very different and distinct ways? Why are the birth narratives in Matthew and Luke completely different? Why is Paul's travel itinerary, as it is told in the book of Acts, different from the travels he describes in his own letters? The gentleman addressing the class stood up and with a paternalistic air said, "Son, if you read the Bible a little bit more carefully you will be amazed to see that there are absolutely no contradictions in the text whatsoever."

"The theory of evolution is just a *theory*." "Fossils were placed in the ground by God when the world was created six thousand years ago." "There was a comet passing by Earth when Jesus was born and that proves that there was a star rising over Bethlehem from the East." When they are not dreaming up harmonizing scenarios such as these, biblical literalists tend to ignore the challenging theories of science, or else they condemn them or blame them on a secular culture that has no reverence for the word and truth of God. Most ironically, they sometimes accept the standards and methods of science and try to show that the Bible is scientifically reliable in all of its claims about the natural world, even while insisting that science itself is mistaken!

Meanwhile, liberal Christians tend to deal with the apparent conflict between scientific claims and biblical claims by gently dismissing the Bible as a creative attempt to explain the natural world supernaturally. It is an admirable exploration of reality by ancient people who didn't know any better. These ancient people did the best they could with the best of what they had. You simply can't expect the writers of the Bible to possess the knowledge we have today; if they did, the Bible would be a very different book. As one parent of a reluctant confirmand once explained to his pastor, "I told my son you have to take the Bible with a pinch of salt. It's just a collection of well-intentioned moral teachings and stories; you can't take them all that seriously."

Both conservative evangelical and liberal attempts to answer the challenges that science and other intellectual endeavors present to the sacred text at the heart of Christianity leave much to be desired. These unsatisfactory answers merely consolidate skepticism among moderates and offer them nothing of lasting value. Dismissing scientific discovery or dismissing the Bible as a source of divine truth is not the way to proceed—not for the church, and certainly not for Dave and Sam.

FAITH AND ACTION: HOW DO I STAND FOR TRUTH?

People don't have to live for very long before they realize that the world does not work the way that any good-hearted person would want it to function. While they may not agree on specifics, liberal, conservative, and evangelical Christians can agree that the world seems broken and in desperate need of fixing. People can be cruel, governments are often corrupt, and the church itself seems mired in dysfunction. So the Christian faith is an active enterprise; it seeks to transform individuals, communities, and institutions for the betterment of God's creation. Sure enough, people often leave church on Sunday morning wondering what they can do to make the world a better place. They start with themselves, but it isn't long before a loving Christian longs to bring about change in the wider society. The ways of the world and the ways of Christ as depicted in the Bible are so often at cross-purposes it can make even the most reticent person want to scream, march, and protest. Divine truth is at stake, and often Christians feel compelled to serve as a public witness for that truth.

Certain Christians gather and picket abortion clinics. Some Christians march in support of gay pride. Other Christians pray outside prison walls to decry capital punishment in hopes of winning a stay of execution. Busloads of Christians make their way to the Mall in Washington, D.C., to be seen and heard. Often enough one group of Christian protesters arrives at a rally only to find another group of Christians who interpret social action oppositely. Christian social action seems merely to duplicate the wider culture's diversity of moral opinion. So what does Christianity add to the cultural mix besides potent rhetoric and religious passion? How can Christians stand together on a given issue when our culture is awash in differing religious and moral opinions? If well-meaning, hardworking people reading the same religious text can't agree on a core set of faith principles to guide social action, then how can we be confident enough in any faith claims to take a stand on any issue?

Conservative Christians typically solve this problem by lumping everyone who disagrees with them into the class of impure lost souls. The so-called Christians among their opponents are apostate—faithless betrayers of Christ. Moderates experience such chest-thumping bullies as transparently insecure and their posturing utterly unconvincing. But moderates are equally worried about liberals whose voice is rarely heard in battles over prominent social conflicts, whose preachers encourage quiet witness, person by person, life by life, day by day. They focus their extensive social action efforts on caring for the homeless and disenfranchised while leaving the task of fighting conservatives over abortion and gay marriage to mostly nonreligious political action groups. A lot of wonderfully loving service gets done by liberals in this quiet way. But does not Jesus' incessant preaching about social justice have a meaningful translation into social witness on high-profile conflicts in our own time? It would be tragic to have to admit that Christianity is useless as a guide for how to organize the moral life of a large and complex society.

Once again, the moderate Christian is stranded. Because of the complexity of the challenges and the inherent divisions in the church, moderate Christians often feel there is nothing they can do to bring the ways of the world and the ways of Christ more closely together. They feel drawn to witness, to take a stand, to speak truth as they have come to know it. But they feel alone, un-supported, confused, and discouraged. As a result, their witness is silenced.

CHAPTER 2

Behind the Questions:
Five Genuine Disagreements

The problem of an ongoing scarcity of truly satisfying moderate answers to deep existential questions can't be wished away. That's because answers from the right and the left are relatively clear and express genuine theological disagreements. We discuss five of these disagreements in terms of the following questions: what is real, what is authoritative, what is the meaning and purpose of history, what is the good, and what is the church?

CONFLICTING VISIONS OF REALITY

Helen believes the Bible is a good book. Actually, she does not think about the Bible often, but she'd tell her pastor it was a good book if he asked. She has a Bible in her house somewhere, but she doesn't read it or study it and probably wouldn't be able to lay her hands on it without a search-and-rescue operation. She listens to Bible stories in church, but she doesn't place much stock in them. Helen doesn't believe in miracles. Jesus didn't *really* walk on water. Mary wasn't *really* a virgin. The world wasn't *really* created in six days. When Helen had breast cancer, she wasn't interested in anyone praying for her recovery. Good care from her doctors and the support of her friends was what she and her family really needed. Helen is a highly educated person. She is pro-choice and opposes the death penalty, she believes in gay rights, and she is an environmental activist.

In truth, Helen liked her church better when it had a more secular way of talking and operating. The new pastor bothers her. He talks about God and Jesus in his sermons all the time and speaks of a world of supernatural powers that she just doesn't accept. Helen would prefer sermons about Jesus as a moral example for us today or about basic human nature and how we can improve ourselves and our society. Helen possesses a determined and confident faith; it is just a faith based on our God-given, grace-filled human potential to be good and to love one another if we try hard and organize society properly. She works selflessly in her church's social programs. She cares for people by cooking meals and holding suffering hands. Though she hasn't read it in a long time, and is not sure which gospel it is in, her favorite Bible story is the one where Jesus explains how God divides people into sheep and goats based not on their beliefs and self-righteous religious professions but on *what they do*. In fact, she has the impression that Jesus was big on action and demanded good works more than right beliefs.

Helen's friend Alex could tell her that the "sheep and goats" story of divine judgment is Matthew 25:31-46. Alex carries his Bible to church and he can quote chapter and verse for many biblical stories. He believes his Bible is a textbook for life, and he wants to understand it to the best of his ability. Alex believes in miracles. If the Bible says the Red Sea parted, it is because God can *really* do that and it *really* happened. The stormy Sea of Galilee was calmed with a word, because Jesus *really* could do that. Jesus healed the sick and the blind, because with God that can *really* happen. When Alex's wife was diagnosed with breast cancer last year, their church gathered around her each week to lay hands on her and pray for her healing. Alex is grateful for the medical attention his wife received, but he believes her remission is a direct result of the miraculous hand of God at work. Alex likes the fact that his pastor preaches from the Bible each week, though he wishes the congregation heard some sermons on traditional family values from time to time. Alex possesses a blazing faith in God's ability to accomplish anything for those who believe. His imagination and day-to-day life are structured by the decidedly nonsecular world of the Bible with its supernatural powers, its divine communications and miracles, its angels and demons.

Helen and Alex sit next to each other in the church choir, or at least they did until Sarah, a local college student, took the alto chair between the two of them. Sarah is new to the church and excited to be a part of the choir. She is cheerful and intelligent, near the top of her college class, and now, in her junior year, she is longing to grow in her faith. She likes both Helen and Alex, though she knows they hold very different beliefs. Helen huffs during the sermons, while Alex quietly whispers "Amen." Sarah has had exactly one conversation about faith with Helen and Alex each, and she is having trouble accepting that Christianity reaches all the way from Alex's spectacular supernatural worldview to Helen's commonsense caring in a world where supernatural powers are nothing more than misunderstandings of the social psychology of evolved human beings. Sarah is mature enough to see the funny side of this situation, but she is not about to try to explain Helen and Alex to each other. So she sits and stands and sings right along with her new friends, wondering what to believe.

These are not caricatures. These are real people, though the names and settings may have been changed. Helen is a liberal of the antisupernaturalist kind. Alex is an evangelical of the passionately supernatural sort. They are both very confident, whereas Sarah isn't sure what to believe. Alex believes in a personal God who can break into our world to effect miraculous change in our lives. He prays unceasingly, in words, with tears and joy, and often on his knees. Sometimes prayer feels almost like a conversation to him. Helen believes that God is less like a supernatural person and more like a principle of perfect love and goodness and feels inspired by God to believe in herself and to work for the rights and welfare of others. She rarely prays in words but has many ways of finding quiet spaces in her life to reflect on God's beauty and on her role in God's creation. Her favorite is walking or sitting in her garden. You couldn't convince Helen that God is a supernatural person, and you couldn't convince Alex that God is anything else.

There are people like Helen, Alex, and Sarah in almost every church. They may not sit next to each other in the choir, but they are seated in the same sanctuary. Some Helen types know the Bible extremely well, and some Alex types don't. Some Helen types are more reflective than active, and some Alex types are more involved in social action than spiritual practices. The details may vary, but the diversity of imaginative worlds is present in the church. The contrast can degenerate into fighting if it is flushed into the open: supernaturalism will be opposed to naturalism, or the sacred will take on the secular. If a church cultivates rhetoric strongly in one direction, then people more at home with the other direction tend to stay quiet because they instinctively recognize the danger to church unity and to their own reputation in the community if they complain. They might not be noisy, but they are still present. Do Alex and Helen have anything in common with one another as faithful Christians? How will they, as members of the supposedly unified body of Christ, reach out in faith to Sarah?

The contrast in imaginative worlds is one of the genuine disagreements that keeps alive the split between liberal and evangelical Christians. Moderates typically have fairly well-defined beliefs themselves, but whatever those beliefs are, most do not want to drive away those whose imaginative worlds clash with theirs. They certainly don't want to be driven away. Many of them will be intensely interested in knowing whether and how a nonsupernaturalist Christian faith can be spiritually lively and true to Jesus Christ and whether and how a supernaturalist faith can take secular knowledge as seriously as it deserves to be taken. But discovering such syntheses requires a journey of living and loving and learning. There are no shortcuts, and jingoistic promises of simple and clear answers are deeply misleading.

CONFLICTING VISIONS OF AUTHORITY

From what do Christians derive authority, and in what do they vest authority? We think there are several sources of authority, in practice, and that the recent history of Christianity in many parts of the world has forced these sources of authority out of harmony, leading to a disorienting, drawn-out, multidimensional conflict. This conflict requires churches and Christians to vest authority in *something*, fully aware that other people vest authority in *something else*. The resulting anxiety naturally drives us to seek a deeper understanding of the conflict.

Authority is a perpetual problem for human beings because it is closely allied with political power. It was just this alliance that led the pilgrims to flee persecution in Europe and colonize North America. For most of the last four hundred years, American Protestantism received its authority from American culture itself. The church was central and is still in many regions of the United States. In fact, for much of our country's history one could assume that a person would receive a fair dose of the Christian medicine just by virtue of being raised in this country, going to American schools, and participating in community events. We have only recently started referring to people as "unchurched." Many Western countries have been Christian cultures for most of their history, and this has meant that cultural prestige has been a source of ecclesial and clergy authority.

In recent decades, the slow tarnishing of the prestige and authority that American culture had bestowed upon the church became obvious. Church and the wider culture experienced greater separation and were more often in conflict than had been the case previously. We all know the stories. A local clergyperson, frustrated by the falling attendance at Sunday morning worship, begins a local crusade to have the town's recreation department stop scheduling sporting events on Sunday mornings. The clergyperson writes impassioned letters to the editor, collects signatures from congregants, and speaks out at town meeting as the pastor of the "church on the hill at the center of town." In the end, the frustrated clergyperson fails in his or her bid to reclaim the Sabbath and concludes that the whitewashed building in the center of town no longer possesses the authority it once conferred on ministers of generations past. People choose soccer over Sunday Sabbath, and for the town the decision is easy: build more ball fields and schedule more games. This sad demonstration has taken place repeatedly in many towns across the United States and in many other countries.

For a brief period of time, in the early seventies and eighties, a charismatic movement swept through many mainline congregations. The charismatic movement recognized the gift of the Holy Spirit, and accompanying vibrant religious experiences, as a legitimate source of authority. However, the churches that participated in this charismatic movement often too narrowly defined the presence of the Holy Spirit. At its best the charismatic movement stirred excitement within previously sedate congregations. At its worst it gave authority only to those who had been "baptized in the Spirit" and were able to demonstrate that gift by speaking in tongues. It was a wonderfully invigorating yet passionately misguided season in the life of the church.

More recently, many congregations, denominations, and church consultant groups have reasserted the Reformation principle that authority derives from the spirit of Christ as encountered in and through the Holy Scriptures. They sought to recall what it means to be a people of the book and, as challenging as it may seem, to live in relationship with the written word of God. With this realization came another: church leaders and denominational bodies recognized that many church people are biblically illiterate. Sermons at mainline churches during the twentieth century were grounded at least as much in current events as in biblical texts, and the Bible was often viewed as a sacred artifact in the sanctuary not to be touched. Meanwhile, in the same period, evangelical churches treated the Bible as the living word of God that needs to be ingested and digested, filling its readers with the sweetness of wisdom (Ezekiel 2:8–3:3) and inspiring them to speak the word of God to others (Ezekiel 3:4ff.).

There is something to be grateful for in the collapse of the church's cultural prestige and dominant social position. It has forced Christians to take responsibility for the way they gain and channel authority rather than simply taking their default attitudes as normative for everyone. This has been a crucial factor in the civil rights movement and the feminist movement; we see ourselves differently partly because our flow of authoritative self-interpretation gets interrupted by awareness of the injustice we perpetuate, deliberately or unintentionally. But the collapse of the church's cultural authority presents problems, too. Christians have scattered in search of the identity-conferring reassurance of divine authority. Some have reified the Bible as the literal verbal communication of God, deserving of ultimate authority and unconditional deference. Others have followed the charismatic impulse to vest authority in intense religious experiences. Some Protestants have vested ultimate authority in the church, inspired by the Roman Catholic approach. A few rely on reason, thinking their way through faith identity questions and feeling a confidence in their cognitive powers that others do not. Some try to strike an artful balance among scripture, tradition, experience, and reason, insisting that all four sources of authority must play a role. These alternative visions of authority are made more important yet simultaneously seem more questionable after the decline of Christianity's authority-conferring cultural prestige.

We suspect most moderate Christians instinctively try to balance sources of authority in the task of articulating Christian identity, beliefs, and practices. Every vision of Christian authority has gone wrong, so moderates tend to steer clear of oversimplified answers to authority questions. Yet holding the center amid contrasting approaches to authority is formidably difficult from a social point of view. Three factors help.

- It is important to educate ourselves about sources of authority to fend off oversimplifications that destroy Christian unity on a whim.
- It is important to develop patterns of discernment that enable a person or a congregation to make decisions that involve balancing sources of authority.
- A determination to love despite differences in perceptions about authority is essential for successfully coping with the confusion that results from admitting diversity of opinion.

Beneath all of the variations in emphasis on sources of authority lies a basic conflict between two recurring attitudes to authority. On the one hand, we have the *tradition-authority* view. On this view, God's Spirit is held to work through groups of people born in and borne up by vast traditions of religious wisdom and spiritual discipline. Such traditions are diffuse explorations of spiritual truth rather than vehicles of definitive and unambiguous divine messages. Authority sufficient for forging a meaningful Christian identity is something people and groups take upon themselves when they engage the divine Spirit through these traditions.

On the other hand, there is the *definitive-authority* view. In this view, God speaks definitively, somehow—perhaps through biblical propositions, through the Pope's infallible teachings on doctrines and morals, through reason and argument, or through the dreams and visions of spectacular religious experiences. When authority is definitive, problems of interpretation and the challenges of discernment are immediately minimized. We need nothing more than plain-sense reading, direct experience, or simple obedience to a religious leader.

The conflict between the tradition-authority and the definitive-authority views is intuitively deeply troubling to Christian moderates. They fear that one of their major priorities—honoring Christ's command that his followers should love one another (John 13:34-35)—cannot compete with the sharpness of the conflict between these visions of authority. In that case, unity of Christian worship can only testify to Christian love on one or the other side of this divide, not across the divide on both sides at once. Is there a way forward?

We believe that the tradition-authority and the definitive-authority views are perhaps best understood not as definite, fixed, and irreconcilable postures but rather as complementary perspectives on religious authority that alternate in dominance through the various stages of life. The child who learns a religious tradition through stories yields to the teenager who longs for and temporarily finds certainty. That same eager absolutist gradually becomes a young adult who teaches a tradition to children using a host of nonliteral, analogical, and symbolic approaches to Bible stories. Thereafter we may find a wise Christian leader searching for definitive identity-forming expressions of faith for the sake of a church in need and eventually an older person surrendering in joy to the mystery of divine authority in human life. The conflict over authority represents a significant lifelong challenge and an opportunity for the deeply curious and determined Christian to plumb the depths of the God-world relationship.

Note that the definitive-authority view is not the same as biblical literalism. They sometimes go hand in hand, particularly in conservative Protestant contexts, but the two ideas must be distinguished carefully. The Catholic Church nicely illustrates the distinction because it combines a definitive, centralized approach to authority with often sophisticated contextual biblical interpretation. Moderates of the liberal-evangelical type will be committed to such nuanced biblical interpretation, which rules out biblical literalism. Yet the definitive-authority view can still have a place in liberal-evangelical churches, held in a balance with the tradition-authority view.

CONFLICTING VISIONS OF HISTORY

We will get at the conflict over the meaning and purpose of history by means of another question, about the role of the church in society. Should the church be a force in the arena of politics? Should the church remain separate from the state and focus solely on individual spiritual development in the hope that an individual's faithful participation in society will change it for the better? There is little agreement between liberals and evangelicals on how to effect social change. In Chapter 7 we will discuss the complex relations among church, state, and the marketplace. At this point we take a more theological approach to the same nest of issues.

The definitive typology for this issue continues to be H. Richard Niebuhr's *Christ and Culture*. In that 1951 book, Niebuhr distinguished five visions of the relationship between Christ and culture:

- Christ against Culture,
- The Christ of Culture,

- Christ above Culture,
- Christ and Culture in Paradox, and
- Christ the Transformer of Culture

This typology was influential because it drew people's attention to the fact that we can and do structure church-society relationships in *a variety of ways*. People are apt to forget this if they are not historians or sociologists. In fact, as Niebuhr himself understood, any historical instance of a relation between the Christian churches and a cultural context implements several if not all of these visions simultaneously in different respects. Moreover, "Christ" is not the same as church, and "culture" is not the same as society, so understanding what these possibilities mean in practice is not straightforward. Still, Niebuhr's typology remains useful as a check on the way we speak theologically and rhetorically about church-society relationships.

Conditions have changed significantly since 1951, and we suspect a simpler distinction has become more important for understanding the liberal versus evangelical conflict, as well as those who are lost in the middle. This distinction pertains to whether or not human cultures and civilization itself can be a means of salvation.

Liberals tend to acknowledge that culture and civilization can be a means of salvation, though never in isolation from divine grace and the work of the Spirit in and through every part of reality. Just as Christians comforting widows and caring for orphans fulfill God's mission, so do societies that do these things through social welfare arrangements. Just as establishing justice on the Earth is a part of the biblical vision of civilization, so too any social or political process that is capable of aiding this end, regardless of religious or cultural affiliation, is potentially salvific.

This reflects a theological interpretation of history that is *developmental* in character, with God working to bring about the kingdom of God on Earth. This developmental perspective persisted even after World War I shattered the late-nineteenth-century liberal illusion of cultural progress being always onward and upward, partly because it has strong biblical credentials. It is linked with an eschatology—a theological theory of the end of history—in which God's kingdom is gradually established on Earth, through a long process of steady transformation, with steps backward and forward along the way. To use one of Jesus' culinary images, the church leavens the lump not merely "in the meantime until God intervenes with a new creation" but "all along the way toward the gradual realization of the kingdom of God."

By contrast, evangelicals tend to regard culture and civilization as a potentially helpful or hurtful context for the drama of salvation but *not salvific in itself*. This view focuses on individual salvation through Jesus Christ rather than corporate salvation through the transformation of human societies. The church leavens the lump only in the sense it helps to keep alive in society the conditions of freedom necessary for spreading the gospel of salvation through Christ. This reflects a theological interpretation of history as a series of *crises* that are opportunities for the saving of souls in the name of Jesus Christ but as having no independent direction or purpose. This view, and the crisis eschatology that tends to go with it, also has strong biblical credentials, thanks to apocalyptic literature, especially in the New Testament. God's consummation of creation consists in destroying the world as it is and creating a new heaven and a new Earth.

None of this implies that liberals are uninterested in individual salvation, though some believe individual salvation is only a by-product of corporate salvation. Nor does it imply that evangelicals are uninterested in the health and welfare of the Earth and its human societies, though some believe it is the domain of Satan and ultimately doomed to destruction. The point we want to stress is that this distinction between the developmental and crisis views of history drives very different conceptions of the way church should relate to society. On the developmental view of history, the church is an essential partner in a wider movement of the Spirit through all of nature and in every human social and individual endeavor. The question of church-culture relations is a strategic one that thoughtful Christians should take with utmost seriousness as a means of realizing God's kingdom on Earth. On the crisis view of history, the church is a shelter from the storm and the doorway to another world of fellowship with God where the former earthly vale of tears is but a distant memory. In this case, the relation between church and society is arbitrary and utterly circumstantial, solely guided, if at all, by the interests of the gospel.

Moderates, as usual, intuitively sense that both of these perspectives must have some truth. It is difficult to believe God created the world in all its vast grandeur and complexity and at the same time tell ourselves God has absolutely no interest in or plan for it apart from saving human souls through Jesus Christ and then destroying it. Likewise, it is difficult to behold the tragic and evil events of the creation without believing a good God would have to be utterly opposed to that which violates the divine holiness and willfully causes the suffering of his creatures. As on other issues, we think the instincts of moderates on this question are on target. Moderates of the liberal-evangelical kind do not have to choose one theological vision of history over the other. The Bible supports both, and it is not given to human beings to know the mysteries of history with godlike clarity. A certain degree of openness and tolerance of diversity of opinion is possible and wise on this point.

CONFLICTING VISIONS OF MORALITY

In Chapter 8 we will discuss textures of moral reasoning between political liberals and conservatives, which we find enormously helpful for understanding conflicting visions of morality. At this point, we anticipate some of these insights in relation to the conflict between liberal Christians and evangelical Christians on moral issues. Religious liberals tend to give free rein to moral intuitions in the domains of suffering and fairness. Meanwhile, they heavily regulate their own moral intuitions pertaining to in-groups and out-groups, to hierarchies, and to purity issues due to their suspicion that such moral intuitions lead to injustice, discrimination, cruelty, and other moral disasters. By contrast, religious conservatives tend to take all of their moral intuitions equally seriously, believing that God gave them their moral feelings for a reason and fearing that the thin moral texture of liberals does too little to protect valuable social norms.

This difference in styles of moral reasoning need not destroy prospects for mutual respect and understanding so long as we understand the difference clearly. But an important practical challenge stands in the way of achieving a concerted moderate Christian moral perspective: moderate liberals and moderate evangelicals have to break free from the narrow ideological agenda of those who wave an extreme political banner and apportion their moral activism to biblical emphases.

For their part, moderate evangelicals have been pigeonholed, or have let themselves become pigeonholed, by conservative evangelical attitudes on a few hot-button issues. Abortion and gay marriage have been, and continue to be, the dominant focus of the religious right's political and media machinery. Meanwhile, though liberal Christians certainly have deep convictions about these issues, they are more likely to disagree among themselves, so they can't raise a unified voice. Rather, liberals tend to speak out on what they can win consensus on, namely, issues of poverty, social justice, debt relief to Third World nations, and environmental protection.

Over the last couple of years, some leading moderate evangelicals—Jim Wallis, Tony Campolo, and Ron Sider, among others—have called for a more deliberate focus of attention and resources on issues of poverty and environmental protection. For example, the Christian Coalition of America and the National Association of Evangelicals attempted in 2005 and 2006 to broaden their agenda to include issues such as combating poverty and environmental destruction. This was met with considerable resistance from within their own ranks. Some conservative evangelical subgroups broke away in protest. In November 2006, Rev. Joel Hunter, the president-elect of the Christian Coalition, turned down the job, saying that he was being blocked from broadening the social action agenda beyond abortion and gay marriage to poverty and the environment—an indication that the most conservative members of the Christian Coalition were winning the fight. Yet the broadening move was welcomed by many evangelicals, and Rev. Hunter's resignation may have had salutary effects within the Christian Coalition itself. In other organizations, including the National Association of Evangelicals, the moderate wing of the evangelical church is finding more success, embracing environmental concerns, and in some cases even beginning to address its troubled past on issues such as slavery, segregation, and women's rights.

Similarly, some moderate liberals are learning to express their dismay over the frequency of abortion while still asserting that government should not legislate over women's bodies. Moderate liberals are also saying biotechnology is truly dangerous even as they recognize its potential for revolutionary medical breakthroughs. This group of moderates is less well organized, but they are learning to speak on controversial issues, not just consensus issues.

Thus, there appears to be growing commonality of purpose between moderate liberals and moderate evangelicals when it comes to issues of societal change. Liberals are learning what evangelicals have known for quite some time: it is essential to have a clear and prophetic voice that is focused and intelligible to the wider society. Moderate evangelicals are learning to value what liberal Christians have long believed: reducing poverty and speaking out for the oppressed are staples of the Christian gospel, and protecting the environment is consistent with that gospel.

The chasm between right and left may be narrowing among moderate Christians on what moral issues should matter. We have no doubt the hot-button issues of our day will continue to accentuate the divide between liberal and evangelical Christians; yet moderate Christians of the liberal-evangelical sort have genuine reason for hope for greater unity of moral purpose.

Conflicting Visions of Church

"I don't go to church to fight; I have enough conflict in my life already. The church should be a place free from politics, agendas, and competing interests." How many church leaders have inwardly groaned at such comments? Somehow there is this misguided belief that once people enter the church all their bad habits, poor communication skills, and questionable judgments should be left at the door, and people should be their true angelic selves. Victims of these grand illusions are often the first to flee the church when people start fighting. Horrified, they proclaim the church to be hypocritical and a poor example of its own teachings.

Everything out there in the wider culture, and every behavioral possibility for human beings, is present somewhere in the church. To believe otherwise is to forget a timeless fact about the church: it is a gathering of sinners. If that weren't bad enough, it is a gathering of sinners led by sinners. The church is as imperfect as the people who make up the community itself. So people disagree in the church, they fight, they get mad, they say things and do things they ultimately regret, they suffer the same slings and arrows as any community in the world.

There is also a distinct difference in the church: it is subject to a commandment of love that most other communities are not, namely, Jesus' commandment: "Love one another as I have loved you. By this all people will know that you are my disciples, that you love one another" (John 13:34-35). Christians are to love one another in all things, so they are to disagree in love and they are to challenge one another in love. Even when their beliefs threaten to wrench them apart, they are to remain bound to one another in love. This means, in principle, that the church should be the perfect place to fight because it is a community whose members vow to love one another without reservation.

Tragically, this vision of love uniting Christians despite disagreements seems as idealistic as thinking that war will end and peace will reign for evermore; it is just not likely. The sad reality is that churches routinely split due to disagreements, churches harbor unhealthy personalities because truth telling seems too difficult, and churches often prefer being polite to being prophetic. On Sundays in many churches, Christians hear sermons and prayers that attack different segments of the church. Evangelical churches rail against liberal Christianity that would sweep aside the biblical witness so that gay and lesbian people can be ordained, marry, and affirmed as beloved children of God *as they are*. At the same time, liberal preachers decry conservative evangelical Christians who wrap themselves in the American flag and proclaim a twenty-first-century gospel of manifest destiny—special divine purpose and protection for the United States.

The demonizing of other Christians is especially troubling to Christians longing and praying for Christian unity. When liberal or evangelical preachers are careless and loveless in their critique of the "other side," they do damage to their own congregations because a host of moderates in every congregation find themselves on awkward middle ground. Moderates typically possess a vibrant faith and a tender care for God's diverse creation. They believe that fighting for their beliefs is important, but inflicting injury on the Christian family is deeply troubling to them. Because they resonate with aspects of both liberal and evangelical theology, their local pastor's attacks on liberalism or evangelicalism leave them feeling on the outside, chastised, and unloved.

At the root of this hostility lies a conflict between ecclesiological ideals: *purity* of the church versus *unity* of the church. Ideals of purity and ideals of unity both seem a bit disconnected with reality in relation to the living church. But moderates need not regard this impracticality as a death sentence for their aspirations of a unified church that is more, rather than less, faithful to Christ's command to love. From our point of view, the key is to redirect aspirations to purity away from transitory debates over moral or doctrinal issues and toward fulfilling the commandment to love one another. Likewise, moderates can redirect their longings for unity away from an idealized harmony of opinion about doctrines and morals and toward mutual support in an unbroken community of worship.

The greatest failure of the Christian ideal of unity is also very simple: it occurs when Christians refuse to gather together in loving fellowship. When a clergyman refuses to participate in his local clergy association because he does not affirm the ordinations of the women who are serving other churches in town, the ideal of unity fails. When denominations refuse to join in communion with one another because of issues of sexuality, the ideal of unity fails. When people within congregations refuse to speak with one another because they are on different sides of a particular issue, the ideal of unity fails. It is when Christians stay at Christ's table and honor Christ's call to love one another that, even in their differences, they are cultivating the very community of which Jesus dreamed, according to the beloved disciple John (John 14–17). It is not necessary to have all the doctrinal answers before meeting and worshiping together. This is purity and unity welded together into a community committed to serving and following Christ. And this defines the aspiration of liberal-evangelical Christians in our time and place.

A Moderate Conclusion

If you are moderate Christian of the liberal and evangelical type, we expect that you will have two questions as you work through this book. One is how the information we present might affect your self-understanding. The other concerns what you should do, practically and positively, about this new self-understanding. We will address these two questions in the conclusion of each part.

First, what new self-understandings might be stimulated by Part I of this book? We think many of you will strongly identify with the haunting questions we discuss in Chapter 1. You may have had the frustrating experience of trying to make sense of one-sided spiritual advice within an evangelical context, feeling that the answers were self-deceptive and defensive. Or you may have had the parallel experience in a liberal context, experiencing the answers as useless for articulating an authentic basis for recognizably Christian faith. If you are particularly unfortunate, you will have been buffeted by contradictory answers from both sides. In all cases, you will sense that something is wrong.

Instead of feeling perpetually frustrated or confused about this situation, it is possible for moderates to see through it and behind it to the profound differences in worldviews that coexist within contemporary Christianity. As we have seen in Chapter 2, the roots of the conflict lie in *disagreements over visions of reality, authority, history, morality, and church.* The underlying worldview conflict that exists within Christianity, and indeed among moderate Christians, is a complicated issue in its own right. Fully grasping it requires dealing with some basic theology and ethics, which is the subject of the companion volume to this one, *Found in the Middle!* If you want to dig deeper, that is a good place to start.

Second, regarding practical and positive next steps, we suggest that moderate Christians should begin talking about worldview conflicts. The benefits of talking about these difficult subjects in a safe environment are considerable.

- Most people learn better when they incorporate an active component such as talking with others alongside passive components such as reading. Talking with others internalizes ideas and makes them available for access later, when we really need them.
- When we talk with one another about worldview conflicts, we discover how diverse we are and learn in practice rather than merely in theory that we actually can love and support one another despite differences in visions of reality, authority, history, morality, and church.
- Talking about difficult faith questions across the generations is profoundly encouraging for all ages, and especially refreshing for young people who may believe that they are the only ones worried about the meaning of faith.
- Talking about faith issues in a safe and supportive environment sounds simple. In practice, however, we know full well how complicated it can be. Flushing these disagreements into the open can make some folk uncomfortable. Christian unity among moderates often seems to depend on finessing worldview disagreements and pretending there is no problem. But we believe there is no shortcut here. The disagreements are real, and moderate Christians need to learn to feel comfortable thinking—and talking—about them if they are to foster the moderate resurgence of which they are a part.

One of us recalls a seminary class in which the professor answered a student's question by quickly sketching this worldview disagreement that pervades contemporary Christianity and showing how it leads to a kind of conflict that seems to go nowhere and gets very frustrating. Several students in the class were stunned. One of them, a young moderate evangelical with a fervent faith, said, "I can't believe I am in my third year of seminary and only hearing this now. This worldview conflict makes sense of so much I have experienced. Why do we hide these fundamental insights when they could make all the difference in helping us understand our lives and future ministries?" We suspect nobody hides these insights on purpose. But they are naturally repressed in order to avoid the terrible disagreements people fear may follow if worldview conflicts are brought into the open. But bringing them into the open at the right time can make a tremendously positive difference in the life of the person who is ready for it.

That's why moderate Christians need to support Christian education for adults as well as for children. We have to engineer environments in which these difficult theological questions can be discussed without fear or recrimination. Such education is a part of serious Christian discipleship. Safe, supportive environments for such discussions rarely spring up spontaneously. Such opportunities are precious, and we have to be intentional about creating and nurturing them.

We close Part I of this book with a final, somewhat troubling thought and a matching concrete suggestion for practical action. Suppose we examine the worldview conflict present in contemporary Christianity through theological study or adult education in congregations. What if coming face-to-face with these differences causes our community to explode? That is the natural fear, isn't it? Can moderates realistically aim to live authentic Christian lives while knowing there are compelling alternative visions of the Christian Way over which people are all too ready to disagree? This is as tough a question as the contemporary church has to face. Indeed, it is the Christian version of the greatest spiritual challenge of our postmodern era: can we understand and love the Other without losing ourselves?

- If the answer is negative, if Christians feel they must both choose one way and decry the other ways as false, then it will be very difficult for them to participate in a liberal-evangelical congregation that prizes unity in love and that derives corporate unity less from doctrinal details and worldviews and more from vibrant worship and caring action. This is a hard but necessary conclusion: Christ-centered radical inclusiveness is not for everyone.

- If the answer is positive, if Christians feel they have it in them to fully appreciate others who think differently, then the possibility for a genuinely bracing form of Christian faith and life begins to emerge.

Many Christian communities strive to realize Christ-centered radical inclusiveness. Many more would launch out in this direction if only they knew how to name their goal and how to reach it. What they most need is supportive resources. That's partly why LiberalEvangelical.org exists. So the practical suggestion is to join the member community of LiberalEvangelical.org. Take resources from the site, share your experiences and ask for advice on the forums, and offer your own ideas and study resources for others to consider. The more moderate Christians embrace the spiritual challenge of learning to claim a radically inclusive form of faith, the more churches will know how to become a lamp on a stand, or leaven in the loaf, to recall two of Jesus' images.

By stressing both diligent Christian education and embracing the spiritual challenge of radical inclusiveness, we are actually pointing to the deepest solution of conflicting worldviews within Christianity. The answer lies fundamentally in a process, not a proposition. Of course, there is a lot to be said about liberal-evangelical theology and ethics, and we do take that up elsewhere. As Jesus' followers understood so clearly from their own experiences with him, however, learning in love brings faith and wisdom where no amount of legalistic doctrine can. In a nutshell, *the only satisfying approach to the challenge of conflicting worldviews within the church is a lifelong journey of radical discipleship, humble learning, and compassionate social engagement.*

What is involved in getting beyond bumper-sticker slogans to lifestyles of radical discipleship, devoted study, and compassionate social engagement? The path of radical discipleship for moderate Christians is not an easy way to walk, and it will never be a wildly popular route because it is demanding and ill-suited to sloganeering. Yet nothing short of this will ever ring true to the discerning moderate Christians for whom we write this book. They have exquisitely sensitive antennae for short-circuited oversimplifications. In the apostle Paul's famous phrase, they want solid food, not milk. That is precisely what the classic wisdom of the Christian tradition, and indeed the wisdom of each of the major religious traditions, offers to those with eyes to see and ears to hear.

PART II

Lost in the Middle?

CHAPTER 3

Neglected Moderates

"Who Speaks for Us?"

At a recent national meeting of a mainline Christian church denomination, a potent debate about gay ordination was underway. The most vocal participants in the debate were on the extremes of the issue, as usual. The conservatives were articulate: they consider homosexuality an abomination based on the authority of biblical testimony. Their God-given moral feelings of disgust confirm this view. They regard ongoing acceptance of homosexual feelings and acts as a sign of an unrepentant sinner, thus making such a person unfit for any church leadership role and, in some cases, unfit even for church membership. The liberals were equally articulate. They argued that the radical inclusiveness of Christ's ministry broke boundaries of prejudice in his day, and following Christ means we should do the same in our day. They applied this to gays, whose profile of sexual attraction, just like that of straight people, is divinely bestowed and irrelevant to whether or not the necessary gifts and graces for ministry are present.

The debate gathered heat as it touched on all of the standard issues: the relevance and authority of the Bible on questions of sexual identity, the extent to which sexual identity is a cultural construction, the alleged possibility of healing the gay "condition," the scientific basis for the naturalness of same-sex attraction, the effects of knowing gay people personally, and the criteria for ministerial ordination. Such public debates rarely go very deep. People are so worried about a close ballot that most operate in the mode of political rhetoric, trying to inspire undecided folk to vote their way. Both extremes believe that minds can't be changed by rational debate on the gay question. The extremes may be right. But it is what happened next that catches our attention.

As the futility and frustration of the debate became more obvious to everyone, one man rose to speak. He said, "I think a lot of us listening to this debate do not hear our views expressed. I have sympathy for some elements on both wings of the argument, I feel profoundly limited by medical and sociological unknowns, I fear that this issue is distracting us from coming to grips with far more centrally biblical social justice challenges, and I am deeply worried about the unity of our church. I want to know why I don't find the extreme positions wholly convincing and why this debate constantly skips over my concerns as it leaps between poles. I believe most of us here feel much the same as I do. Who will speak for us?"

Situations akin to this one have occurred repeatedly in relation to many controversial issues from church polity to biblical inerrancy and from abortion to war. In every such polarized debate, many people feel lost in the middle and fervently wish that someone would speak for them. Those in the silent moderate majority usually don't fully identify with either articulate extreme, and they see some good points on all sides. Most of all, they are unwilling to sacrifice Christian unity prematurely over a fight that seems to be more about Christian identity than whatever the surface issue is.

Who speaks for those who feel lost in the middle? Those on the left and right are richly blessed with guidance and support. But who helps those in the messy middle understand their moral and religious convictions? Who gives voice to their principles and teaches them how to express themselves?

We believe that there is profound wisdom among moderate Christians but that it takes some effort to uncover it and name it. Unfortunately, the razor-sharp rhetoric of extremes, like the television sound bite and the radio shock jock, sets a low standard for the complexity of public debate. People in the middle sometimes feel dull-minded and morally paralyzed because they can't compete with the simple clarity of extremes. But these folk are neither unintelligent nor indecisive nor uncommitted. In fact, they often exhibit impressive sophistication in their moral and theological reasoning. Most choose to stand in the middle not out of an aversion to conflict but because their instincts tell them that the simplicity of the extremes misses the mark. Surprisingly, "lost in the middle" moderates often feel both neglected and confident.

A Demographic Profile

Who are these "lost in the middle" people? Do we know anything about them and what matters to them? Because they are caught between extremes, we might assume they are always tossed into the "everyone else" category, whose hodgepodge members have no focused identity and little in common. But survey data give shape to the messy midlands.

Numbers: Political Moderates

Let's begin with politics, which is what survey data handle most easily. Political moderates are a large group in the United States. On the questions of political ideology, surveys repeatedly report that almost half of Americans identify themselves as moderates, with most of the rest divided between conservatives and liberals. Surveys have to be read with a grain of salt, but similar numbers keep coming up so there is reason to take them seriously. For example, the 2004 ABC News Poll on Religion and Politics returned 21 percent liberal, 42 percent moderate, and 36 percent conservative. The 2001 ABC News-Beliefnet Poll returned 23 percent, 39 percent, and 30 percent on the same categories, and the 2005 ABC News-Washington Post Poll yielded 46 percent moderates.

The more refined categories of the Pew Research Center's 2002 Religion and Public Life Survey show that political moderates are the dominant group.

Very liberal	3.8%
Liberal	13.2%
Moderate	40.0%
Conservative	31.5%
Very conservative	5.7%
Don't know/Refused	5.7%

Table 1: The Pew Center's 2002 Religion and Public Life Survey: profile data on political ideology

The National Opinion Research Center's 2004 General Social Survey used even more refined categories to make discriminations within the liberal wing and the conservative wing.

Extremely liberal	3.4%
Liberal	9.0%
Lean to liberal	11.4%
Moderate	37.1%
Lean to conservative	16.0%
Conservative	16.6%
Extremely conservative	4.2%
Don't know/Refused	2.3%

Table 2: 2004 General Social Survey: profile data on political ideology

These results suggest that, when the wording of survey questions gives them the chance, almost two-thirds of Americans will identify themselves as moderates or as moderates who lean a little right or left. This is not news. Political campaigns have always been out to capture the hearts and minds of moderate Americans. Seeing the numbers reminds us that moderates are a large and influential group in U.S. politics.

Numbers: Religious Moderates

Religious moderates are also a large group. For example, in the coarse categories of the 2004 General Social Survey, roughly 39 percent of Americans identify themselves as theological moderates. The alternatives were fundamentalist and liberal, suggesting that the question needs to be asked more carefully. Others have done so.

George Barna founded the Barna Research Group in 1984 to conduct market research at the intersection of faith and culture. Now called the Barna Group, their surveys are notable for paying close attention to the difference between Christian self-identification and the actual content of people's beliefs. While we consider some of Barna's definitions a bit contrived, their strategy is extraordinarily helpful for getting behind vague labels and achieving a clearer profile of Christians in the United States.

Barna divides the population into five faith segments. Rather than asking merely for religious self-identification, the Barna surveys ask about people's beliefs and practices and then classify them into one of the five segments accordingly. As of 2002, the data we are analyzing, a whopping 41 percent of Americans were "born-again Christians." That's about 100 million people. The percentage has varied only slightly since the Barna Group began using this methodology in 1991 and has remained fairly constant through to 2006. In the Barna world, born-again Christians believe that their eternal destiny is salvation by God's grace through a personal faith relationship with Jesus Christ.

The born-again group contains evangelical and nonevangelical subgroups, with the 80 million nonevangelical born-agains being about four times as numerous as the evangelical born-agains. The 20 million Americans who are *evangelical* born-agains on the narrow Barna definition uphold key theological doctrines such as the total accuracy of the Bible's teachings, Jesus' perfect sinlessness, the personal reality of Satan, and the impossibility of salvation through good works alone. That is, they maintain belief in the key elements of a supernatural biblical story of salvation that treats God as an omnipotent, omniscient, active personal being who is in control of the world and implements a plan for salvation by means of the incarnation and sacrifice of his only son Jesus Christ to overcome the power of the devil and the effects of sin.

In Barna's groupings, the roughly 80 million Americans who are *nonevangelical* born-agains depart from this story in some vital way. We are very interested in this group of people because we think that many of them deem the conservative evangelical Christian narrative less than completely compelling, just as they find the liberal dilution of the story as a "true myth" deeply upsetting.

Barna also assigns 44 percent of Americans to the category of "notional Christians." This refers to people who describe themselves as Christians but do not qualify as born-again because they are not sure about salvation, because they believe salvation is based on good deeds, or because (and this is true for the large majority of this subgroup) they think that salvation depends only on God's grace and does not require a personal relationship with Jesus Christ. We are also interested in this group. The Barna perspective on authentic Christian faith, as expressed in George Barna's publications and commentaries, tends to dismiss these people as not serious Christians; even the name "notional Christian" conveys this valuation. But we think many of them have deep religious commitments but feel alienated from the confident world of conservative Christianity.

Barna's remaining two categories are people of non-Christian faiths (7 percent) and agnostics, atheists, or nonreligious people (8 percent). Here are the numbers in summary form.

Evangelical born-again Christians	8%
Nonevangelical born-again Christians	33%
Notional Christians	44%
People of other faiths	7%
Agnostics/Atheists/Nonreligious people	8%

Table 3: Barna Group's Five American Faith Segments (2002)

Labeling Realities

Most people use the label "evangelical" far more generously than the Barna Group does. Barna's research demonstrates that most of the 41 percent of American adults who feel comfortable describing themselves as "evangelical" actually believe things that would make the 8 percent he calls strict evangelicals distinctly uneasy. Similarly, a far higher percentage of people (53 percent) describe themselves as "theologically conservative" than their actual beliefs suggest is appropriate. By contrast with such inflated labels, the group of people self-identifying as "born again" in Barna's surveys is about the same size (39 percent) as the group meeting Barna's definition of the term (41 percent). Experience-based labels seem less subject to distortion than doctrine-based labels.

To accommodate these labeling realities, we think it is clearest to speak of Barna's "evangelicals" as "strict evangelicals" or "conservative evangelicals" and to allow the term "evangelical" the broad semantic range it has traditionally enjoyed. We will adopt this usage in what follows, even when discussing research from the Barna Group.

The 2006 Baylor Religion Survey cleverly presented subjects with a range of labels and asked them to say both whether they *identify* with the label and whether the label is the *best description* of their religious identity. This approach showed that people often feel dissatisfied with standard labels even when they identify with them. Presumably, this is due to media and academic abstractions and to the way labels are used by their most prominent advocates. The popular impression given by the rhetoric of high-profile debates—namely, a simple religious landscape with clearly defined poles containing vast blocks of opposed Christians—appears to be quite wrong. People in the United States are thinking for themselves about religion much more than usually suggested by media caricatures. Here are the numbers.

Religious Identity Label	% identifying with label	% saying label is best description
Bible-Believing	47.2%	20.5%
Born Again	28.5%	18.6%
Mainline Christian	26.1%	12.9%
Theologically Conservative	17.6%	5.3%
Evangelical	14.9%	2.2%
Theologically Liberal	13.8%	9.1%
Moral Majority	10.3%	1.7%
Seeker	8.5%	3.9%
Religious Right	8.3%	1.2%
Fundamentalist	7.7%	1.0%
Charismatic	7.3%	0.3%
Pentecostal	5.8%	1.7%
None of These	—	21.8%

Table 4: Baylor Religion Survey on religious identity labels (2006)

What can we draw from these surveys? They indicate that moderate Christians with some sympathies for both evangelical and liberal Christianity are a *large group*, just as political moderates are the dominant political grouping. That ought to comfort a lot of people because the blustering rhetoric of our time suggests a very different picture.

Our target audience—the folk who sometimes feel lost in the middle—are in this large containing group of moderate Christians and probably dominate it. Relative to Barna's groupings, the containing group is the majority subgroup within the non-strict evangelical born-again Christians *who take the Bible seriously but not always literally,* plus the large majority of the notional Christians *who retain a strong interest in keeping Jesus Christ at the center of their faith.* This group includes many charismatic, Pentecostal, and mainline denominational Christians. It includes a fair proportion of the dedicated Christians who maintain no relationship or only a loose relationship with a local church. It includes about equal numbers of Democrats and Republicans. But it excludes conservative evangelicals and fundamentalist Christians for whom biblical literalism is necessary for recognizing the authority of the Bible. And it excludes secularized liberals for whom Jesus Christ is an optional aspect of Christian faith. For want of a better encompassing term, we call everyone in the middle grouping "religious moderates" or "Christian moderates."

Characteristics of Religious Moderates

What do we know about this large group of religious moderates? We know quite a lot, actually. For some years, the Barna Group has investigated the moral convictions, religious practices, and theological beliefs of people in the five faith segments. Table 5 presents the summary, using our categorizations rather than Barna's. Remember the moderates we are writing for are sizable subgroups within the "Other born-again Christians" and "Not born-again Christians" faith segments. As expected, the two containing groups for our religious moderates are stuck in the middle of the conservative evangelical Christians and the rest in almost all categories. This table takes a bit of work to absorb but it is worth studying closely.

THE REASSERTION OF MODERATE CHRISTIANITY

Moderate Christians are not remaining passive. In fact, there is evidence that they are sick of being the marginalized majority and are starting to reassert themselves. We are not aware of formal sociological survey data on the reassertion of moderate Christians and would love to see it. We think the fundamental power source for this reassertion is worry that the bitterness of cultural fighting is becoming more dangerous than the substantive issues people fight over. Moderates are slow to move and tend to be disorganized when they do—more like a fabulously fat walrus on dry land than a sleek, conservative evangelical cheetah running across the savanna. But the sheer number of moderates gives them clout, and some of them feel ready to use that clout.

	Conservative evangelical born-again Christians	Other born-again Christians	Not born-again Christians	Not Christian religion	Agnotic, Atheist, or nonreligious
Total in population (2002)	8%	33%	44%	7% .	8%
Political Views					
Mostly conservative on social issues	70%	37%	25%	12%	12%
Registered Republican	58%	35%	26%	11%	15%
Moral Convictions					
Bible or church grounds moral decisions	68%	27%	11%	8%	3%
Absolute moral truth exists	58%	27%	15%	17%	10%
Homosexuality is morally unacceptable	95%	59%	38%	27%	20%
Cohabitation is morally acceptable	10%	42%	65%	82%	92%
Movies with explicit sex are acceptable	12%	33%	54%	75%	79%
Having an abortion is morally acceptable	4%	24%	38%	67%	71%
Religious Practices					
Read from the Bible in past 7 days	86%	53%	24%	17%	9%
Attended church service in past 7 days	80%	58%	36%	14%	9%
Theological beliefs					
Strongly disagree with "Satan is not a living being but a symbol of evil"	100%	26%	15%	20%	15%
Strongly disagree with "On Earth, Jesus Christ was human and committed sins"	100%	53%	27%	20%	20%
Strongly disagree with "The Holy Spirit is a symbol of God's presence but not a living entity"	86%	22%	11%	20%	13%

Table 5: Barna Group, "A Comparison of Five Faith Segments"

What is their message to the noisy extremes? Settle down and remember the Christian basics about loving enemies and placing service to others ahead of gaining power over them!

Comedian Jon Stewart is best known for being host of Comedy Central's satirical current affairs program *The Daily Show*. In 2004, he triggered an episode that has become symbolic of moderate reassertion in politics. Stewart appeared on CNN's debate program *Crossfire* and attacked hosts Tucker Carlson and Paul Begala for hurting America with their polarized approach to political debate, calling it "dishonest" and "partisan hackery." Shortly thereafter newly appointed CNN president John Klein canceled *Crossfire*, presumably for many reasons. But he said publicly that he agrees with Stewart's point of view and wants to support an approach to the news more substantive than the ridiculous shouting matches for which *Crossfire* was justly infamous. Political moderates everywhere celebrated a victory for decency and common sense and rejoiced that someone was committed to lifting the quality of public debate.

Political moderates also asserted themselves in the 2006 U.S mid-term elections, wresting control of both houses of Congress from the Republicans and handing it to the Democrats. This may have been done more as punishment for Republicans than with any real hope that Democrats would make a huge difference. Or perhaps it was mainly a vote against President George W. Bush's foreign policy. But it was done nonetheless and stands a stern reminder to complacent politicians that the political middle in the United States is large and can direct their anger toward any party if it misbehaves or displays incompetence.

Religious moderates are also on the move in American politics. One sign of this is progressive evangelical Jim Wallis's 2005 call to metaphorical arms in *God's Politics: Why the Right Gets It Wrong and the Left Doesn't Get It*. The huge reception of this book showed how dissatisfied progressive evangelicals are with a Christian vision of politics that neglects the biblical heritage of social justice.

Then there is the "greening" of evangelicals, as they slowly catch on to the importance of ecological stewardship, despite their suspicion of the politics and theology of environmentalists. For the older group of evangelical leadership, environmental worries are Satan's carefully crafted distraction from the principal task of evangelism. But the authority of the seasoned evangelical warriors has proved insufficient to block moderate evangelicals from asserting their concerns for the environment, often under the heading of "creation care" or "stewardship."

Another very public sign that evangelicals with moderate progressive agendas are on the move is the reception of David Kuo's 2006 *Tempting Faith: An Inside Story of Political Seduction*. A conservative Christian, Kuo is an experienced political operative who served as special assistant to George W. Bush from 2001 to 2003 and was second-in-command of the administration's Office of Faith-Based Initiatives. His book is a sincere insider's perspective on the way Christian interests in social justice always play second, third, or tenth fiddle to political realities. It includes some striking revelations about the cynical attitude of some in the Bush administration to conservative evangelical Christians, welcoming them with warm embraces and dismissing them behind their backs as "kooks." Many evangelical commentators took this book very seriously as confirmation of the hard fact that authentic Christianity in league with politics inevitably compromises itself and is perpetually vulnerable to exploitation. The fulfilling of the biblical vision of social justice seems more important than ever to these Christians, but they may have to go about it differently.

An instance of moderate reassertion that embraces both politics and religion is Barack Obama's public profile: his 2004 election to the senate, his books, especially *The Audacity of Hope: Thoughts on Reclaiming the American Dream* (2006), his capture of the 2008 Democratic presidential nomination, and his election as president on November 4, 2008. This is a politician who inspires strong interest among moderates in both Republican and Democratic parties, as well as independents. Obama's success is due primarily to the grassroots support network that has sprung up around his message of shared American values, the constructive transformation of political debate, and the realignment of America's role in world affairs. He clearly realizes what this means: political moderates are longing for a new voice that gets beyond partisan bickering and blinkered policy debates, and religious moderates want to identify wholeheartedly with the faith commitments and moral convictions of a politician. What that means in practice remains to be seen for President Obama; Washington, D.C., is not an easy place to change. But it is the nature of the phenomenon itself that we are pointing to: it is a moderate message of unity that rejects the polarized rhetoric of extremes.

There are numerous initiatives among religious moderates actively seeking to resist political and theological polarization. They look to reclaim a classically Christian sense of a spiritually compelling and socially potent faith that is also diverse and open. We have studied a number of these moderate Christian movements and are impressed with the imagination and commitment of their leaders. Here a couple of examples.

Del Brown grew up in a conservative evangelical family and church environment. Along with the formative experiences of family and schooling, he invested himself in the church, becoming intensely involved in Bible study and evangelistic outreach. With time and experience, the certainties of his youth came to seem overbaked, and yet his passion for the Christian faith remained strong. Formal study of the Bible, church history, theology, and ethics deepened his Christian commitment to the point that he became quite comfortable with the pluralism of Christian belief and practice. In due course he became a professor and taught in both secular university and seminary contexts. Brown's last appointment before retiring was dean of the Pacific School of Religion in Berkeley, California. There, in 2006, he founded The Progressive Christian Witness, a Web resource aiming to strengthen the public voice of socially progressive Christians. In the article "Invitation to Christian Conversation," Brown and his colleagues write,

> Christians in every part of the country are organizing and calling for a renewal of the progressive Church. Many of these people are heirs to liberal Christian traditions. A number of them stand in the heritage of evangelical and conservative Christianity. Some defy categories. But all say that the health of the nation and the world—to say nothing of the integrity of the

nation and the world—to say nothing of the integrity of the Church—requires a more effective progressive Christian witness in America today.

We agree. We think The Progressive Christian Witness is a commendable project. Brown's journey to this point in his life is inspiring. Just as when he was a young Christian, he is still striving to nurture the faith of Christians and to make a difference in the world.

If Brown's work at the Pacific School of Religion reaches into the vast middle spaces from a roughly liberal perspective, then Jim Wallis's work at Sojourners springs from essentially evangelical roots. Despite the attendant theological differences, their conceptions of the importance of the Christian gospel for social justice are remarkably similar. Like Brown, Wallis was raised in an evangelical family. As a youth he refused to accept the racial segregation of American society and its war-oriented foreign policy, and so he invested himself in the civil rights movement and antiwar protests. His commitment to social justice flowered into an intentional community and a magazine. Founded in 1971, the magazine has been known as *Sojourners* since 1975. The movement's website offers the following bracing invitation:

> Rooted in the solid ground of prophetic biblical tradition, Sojourners is a progressive Christian voice that preaches not political correctness but compassion, community, and commitment. We refuse to separate personal faith from social justice, prayer from peacemaking, contemplation from action, or spirituality from politics.
>
> Sojourners includes evangelicals, Catholics, Pentecostals, and Protestants; liberals and conservatives; blacks, whites, Latinos, and Asians; women and men; young and old. We are Christians who want to follow Jesus, but who also sojourn with others in different faith traditions and all those who are on a spiritual journey. We reach into traditional churches but also out to those who can't fit into them. Together we seek to discover the intersection of faith, politics, and culture. We invite you to join, to connect, and to act. Welcome to the community.

How can any Christian serious about the biblical vision of justice, mercy, and humility say no to that?

Between the older Sojourners and the younger Progressive Christian Witness, hundreds of moderate movements have sprung up, and they are starting to become aware of one another. Each has a slightly different mission, but all are committed to resisting the polarization of political debate and the forced trivialization of Christian diversity into black-and-white terms. And most have a well-defined social agenda somewhere in the moderate range that is deeply influenced by a biblical vision of social justice, led by the principle of radical inclusiveness as defined and inspired by Jesus' life and ministry.

CHAPTER 4

Culture Wars and Religion

SEMINARY STYLES AND CONGREGATIONAL IDENTITY

If there is one thing North American Christians at the beginning of the twenty-first century *think* they understand, it is the divide between liberal and evangelical in the church. Polarized ecclesiastical publications tell their stories from the left or from the right, constructing competing denominational identities that clash in the consciousness of members. If a denomination has only one important publication, it avoids the issue with quaint desperation, trying to keep everyone happy. Mainstream media relentlessly draw our attention to "culture wars" and give detailed coverage to high-profile court cases on controversial moral issues, with religious viewpoints front and center.

To get a sense for how this works in the seminary context, consider the following story, which accurately depicts one particular situation but also represents what commonly happens in theological schools.

Harry and Jean are seminarians who face this liberal versus evangelical conflict head-on in theology and Bible classes where they have to find their way in what sometimes feels like hostile territory. Jean can't grasp why seminary classes on the Bible do not take literary and historical criticism of the Bible for granted and get into the wonderful details, which are so exciting to her. And she can't fathom why her taste for theological pluralism is confronted in class by fellow students insisting that theology should be done one way and one way only, for the sake of church identity, loyalty to sacred tradition, and the "truth."

Meanwhile, Harry feels increasingly desperate as his view of the Bible's authority is challenged over and over again. Church history classes present the massive pluralism of Christian belief and practice, forcing him to recognize his formerly unquestioned sense of Christian identity for what it is: a local identity that is one of many in the history of Christianity. These experiences cause both Harry and Jean to wonder whether the ecumenical ideal of spiritual unity among all Christians is a feasible goal and whether the very idea of Christianity is coherent when the full diversity of Christians and churches is taken into account.

Seminary hallways and common rooms are opportunities for like-minded people to cluster for support and companionship. Occasionally student meetings and late-night discussions become forums for intense arguments among differently minded seminarians. It is in this context that Harry and Jean get to know one another and get used to fighting. But it is not easy to interpret what goes on in those exchanges. Are they seeking mutual understanding? Trying to impose an agenda on each other? Sorting out their own identities and testing their commitments? All of the above? Sometimes their discussions have a loving tone despite the tensions. Other times they turn almost hostile. Harry and Jean have had to apologize to each other more than once.

Entire seminaries have theological "cultures," at least by reputation. Well-intentioned mentors fearfully advise future seminarians to "steer clear of school X because it is too liberal and will destroy your faith" or "to stay away from school Y because it is too evangelical and hostile to legitimate diversity of opinion." In practice, seminary life is always more textured, but the cultural realities are undeniable. Polarization is most obvious to those students and faculty who sense they are not in the dominant ideological culture. The pressure to conform rather than rock the boat can be extraordinarily frustrating given that seminary is supposed to be a time of authentic spiritual formation as well as academic learning and professional development. Even worse, polarization induces bad behavior in seminaries, with like-minded people bonding together by belittling those with different views behind their backs.

Pastors face the conflict, too. Churches, like seminaries, have cultures. Church reputations are often skin-deep, but the culture of a church is a deeper, almost intangible thing. A wise pastor we know quickly gained a sense for the real pluralism within a congregation upon arriving to begin ministry there. That pluralism came in the form of multiple pressures to meet stated needs in particular ways. "We like biblical preaching." "We like social-justice preaching." "We like to hear about our pastor's personal faith journey from the pulpit." "We want a healing service." "We want more opportunities for social action." Most comments struck him as defined by the polarized theological conflict in the wider culture. Do the squeaky wheels get the grease? Our pastor friend worried about all the people who don't come right out and say what they expect from their minister. What do they really think? What do they truly need? All wise pastors keep in mind that their obligations as ministers extend beyond just satisfying the desires of congregational "customers."

Each congregation's history and circumstances help to produce these frustrations and longings and influence the way people give voice to them. To gain a deeper sense for the character of the congregation, this pastor had to investigate its history. He did that through a series of conversations with revered members having long memories of the church's development. He then wrote up what he discovered in a kind of informal history of the congregation and presented it in various church venues. What happened next was very special. Most church members stopped clamoring for his attention. Most surrendered their fearful turf-protecting forms of communication with their new pastor and started to take their bearings from their own church's congregational history instead. The polarized character of the complaints and appeals changed into a celebration of a church narrative everyone could embrace. Not everyone was swept up in the enthusiasm, of course. But many church members discovered a deeper church culture all their own lying beneath the polarized surface fights.

Leadership transitions in congregations do not always work out this constructively. Alongside the pressure to "be this or that for us," ministers have to endure the families that leave, disappointed with one or another aspect of the new ministry. Another pastor friend of ours reports that he routinely hears (usually indirectly, of course) contradictory criticisms. "You're too conservative for us." "You don't take the Bible literally enough for me." He has had to endure semiorganized blocks of parishioners who seem to spend more time sniping at his ministry in the shadows than in building up the church community in worship and Christian practice. All this is incredibly frustrating, enormously stressful for spiritual identity, and a serious challenge to our friend's sense of call.

Sadly, congregational identity politics often induce such intense stress on newly minted ministers that they leave the ministry feeling burned out, beaten up, and betrayed by the church they love. Research shows that this occurs more often for women in ministry: in addition to the generic challenges of church politics, women ministers have to deal with some parishioners who are uncomfortable accepting the authority of a woman in the pulpit and in church administration. Indeed, entire denominations continue to reject the very idea of ordained women clergy.

CONFLICTING CARICATURES

Beneath these all-too-familiar conflicts and tensions supposedly lies a fundamental split between liberal and evangelical Christians. In theology and biblical interpretation, in seminary styles and church cultures, liberals and evangelicals know they are different from one another and feel the differences sharply. Inevitably, caricatured readings of the "other" come to life.

Caricature #1: Liberal Christianity is a tangle of habits that, like a parasitic vine, chokes the very life out of the church upon which it grows. The good news is an intellectually tortured and ultimately incoherent story about, well, something to do with love. It is the religion of the upper classes, the socially and economically privileged, the bleeding-heart activists seeking economic and social justice for the less fortunate. It has little emotional power to draw people together in life-transforming ways because people in this milieu are afraid of their own psychological shadows and don't know how to get emotional. It is old-fashioned, sensible, and bores young people to tears. It sends many folk right out the church door, never to return, once they see what they are asked (or not asked) to believe and do in the name of liberal Christianity. It is treasured by many faithful Christians the way lovely suburban neighborhoods are treasured but is shrinking in its relatively small corner of global Christianity.

Caricature #2: Evangelical Christianity is all about passionate proclamation. Its gospel story is clear in the way bedtime stories for children are clear. It requires buying into an old-fashioned worldview that has little to do with the modern world we inhabit and love to complain about. It is confident in an afterlife where everything bad about this world gets put right but that just brings comfort to the confident while undermining effective social activism. It promotes life-transforming experiences that change people's behavior patterns and make for large and bustling churches, but is perpetually naive about the way that strongly bonded groups always produce spectacular life changes, regardless of the gospel preached. Best of all, evangelical enthusiasm lets you take your feelings out for a spin while giving your brain a good long rest. It boasts a countercultural moral posture, but on many economic and moral issues it is a premier instance of culture Christianity. It is famous for sheep stealing and overblown numbers, but there is no question that evangelical forms of Christianity are expanding all over the world.

The caricatures are potent. Just like cartoon drawings, they distort prominent features to make a point. As with most caricatures, there must be an opportunity for laughter here somewhere. If we could find our way to a humorous appreciation of these caricatures as affectionate teasing rather than hostile character assassination, we would all be significantly better off. But most of the time, that lightness of heart, that companionable modesty seems impossibly distant. *It requires the kind of self-acceptance and spiritual maturity that places love ahead of power and responsibility to others ahead of defending our rights.* In practice, some seminary students and ministers and congregations feel impatient around these issues, and harshness and arrogance from both left and right are the result.

Interestingly, most African Americans do not readily interpret their faith experience and church life in liberal-versus-evangelical terms. One of our African American colleagues describes the phenomenon this way: "We African Americans don't usually peg ourselves as liberal or evangelical. We are Christians, and our identity turns more on social action to represent the kingdom of God. In fact, most African American Christians are unwilling to tip their hand about what they really believe because they know it might be controversial. That makes identifying progressive African American pastors quite difficult." There is a complex history that helps to explain this hesitancy to be transparent about beliefs. We suspect unity within an African American church is extremely important to its members because the common heritage of slavery and racism is more definitive for identity than any disagreements over theology or politics. Predominantly white congregations do not feel the same obligation to one another. They can afford the luxury of disagreement in a way that most African American congregations cannot.

Despite these heritage-driven differences, the theological and worldview disagreements we have discussed exist within African American churches, albeit usually quietly. They also exist under the radar within evangelical megachurches whose identity centrally depends on the personality of a dynamic pastoral leader. They even exist within Catholic congregations, where participation in the Mass centrally defines what it means to be religious. The social identity of some churches allows the conflicts to surface, whereas in other churches they remain submerged. But they are usually there. After all, these worldview disagreements are a crucial and unavoidable aspect of our postmodern cultural and religious environment.

MUTUAL ATTRACTION

As we have seen, there is a rather large group of moderate Christians who feel they do not fit either caricature, even if their self-labeling and church affiliation places them on one side or the other. Among these moderates are many who feel worried, frustrated, disaffected, or bored. These folk look longingly outward from the camp of their nominal affiliation toward the other camp and want some of what it has, fundamentally because they sense the other within themselves. There are plenty of such people on both sides.

What do moderates in liberal contexts want that evangelicals have? To put our answer first in crass terms, they envy the numbers, the money, and the sheer institutional buoyancy of most evangelical churches. More profoundly, they thirst for biblical preaching that is comprehensible, relevant, educational, and inspiring. They covet the spiritual energy of dynamic music and passionate worship. They long for those small group meetings where people reach out in compassion to one another and come away feeling truly understood and supported. They crave explicit expectations that translate the cost of being a Christian into moral, financial, and spiritual terms.

They would not want to surrender their freedom to interpret the Bible according to their conscience, as guided by critical scholarship. They would not be eager to embrace an authoritarian form of religion, nor shake-and-bake spirituality, nor flat-footed theological responses to life's terrible moments of suffering. They would never surrender their passion for social justice, their commitment to the transformation of social conditions affecting the poor, or their love of learning and the literate ideal of human freedom passed down through the liberal tradition of politics and religion. They might not change the way they vote. But they would prize an energetic Christian community with a comprehensible message and the power to help them forge close relationships, transform recalcitrant habits of thought and behavior, and inspire them to an intimate relationship with God.

What do moderates in evangelical contexts want from liberals? Freedom to be themselves. They want freedom from arbitrary authorities who impose convention in place of reason and stamp out creativity and originality. They long for freedom to think and feel across the range of life's complexities, within and beyond the core narrative of their own evangelical community. They seek *freedom from* social coercion in which their group's way is the only way and *freedom to* see the group from the outside, through the eyes of the marginalized or ignored. As much as they love their core evangelical message, they crave *freedom from* its sameness and rigidity—and *freedom to* make it more realistic, more flexible, more persuasive. As much as they love the energy of close-knit church life, they yearn for *freedom from* its intrusiveness—and *freedom to* have the privacy of their thoughts and feelings honored in a less invasively bonded community.

They would not want to give up their personal relationship with Jesus, their confidence in God's revelation in the Bible, their belief that divine wisdom is more important than cultural wisdom, or their passionate commitment to salvation as the ultimate goal of human life. They might not change the way they vote either. But they are tired of moral intolerance, doctrinal rigidity, and monochromatic spirituality. They want to submit to God alone, and not any human institutional authority, so they want to decide for themselves what to believe and how to act, at prayer, in worship, and through dialogue with a vastly complex and internally diverse tradition.

Avoidance or Engagement?

If some get angry when they feel caricatured, and some feel they half-fit both caricatures at once, some others are utterly sick of thinking and talking about conflicting liberal and evangelical religious world pictures. Just using the words "liberal" and "evangelical" sometimes brings to the surface bad feelings and knee-jerk reactions. They just want to get past it all. To dwell on these bogey words is to reify the very caricatures that Christians need to transcend, they say. They demand new words and new ideas because the old ideas are dead and the old words poisonous.

We sympathize. And we'd like to accommodate. There is no question what we advocate for in this book has more to do with combining long-standing Christian wisdom with cutting-edge knowledge about the dynamics of religious groups than with labels. We do not *need* the words "liberal" and "evangelical" to explain the way that moderate Christians have distinctive access to a radical form of faith and church life. Yet steering around controversial labels feels wrong to us. The people we want to reach are already interpreting their worlds in terms of these labels, and they are historically vital.

Despite the clarity of the rhetoric, as the survey data show, only a minority of Christians are neatly liberal or evangelical. Many Christians and congregations instinctively sense that "liberal" and "evangelical" belong together in some ways. They long to find a way to honor what they love in both. For them, this conflict is like having divided loyalties in a civil war: victory by either side can't possibly be a good thing, and they just want the fighting to stop. But they are also suspicious of new words and phrases that just repackage without truly engaging the problem. To them, avoidance just lets something fester, and jingoistic relabeling seems scatterbrained and fainthearted.

We notice these feelings in many of our parishioners and church friends, our seminary students and ministerial colleagues. Maybe it is just a bicoastal issue, a blue-state issue, or a Protestant issue. We doubt it. And the survey results don't support this interpretation. The desire to unite the compassionate openness and social activism of liberal Christianity with the corporate magnetism and spiritual fervor of evangelical Christianity comes not from politics or geography but from spirituality and common sense. It strikes us that many Christians, and especially seminary students, ministers, and lay church leaders, long for a deeper understanding of the problem. They are willing to undertake the sociological, theological, and spiritual exercise involved in winning that deeper understanding. It is on behalf of such people that we refuse to skip over the "liberal" and "evangelical" labels.

We need to mount a direct attack on the religious rhetoric of our cultures and churches and on the conflicting narrative worlds that sustain it. Moreover, we ourselves do not want to give up these precious words. They might seem bogey words right now, but it was not always so and need not be so in the future.

Here's the crux of the issue. We began this chapter by saying that most North American Christians at the beginning of the twenty-first century *think* they understand the divide between liberal and evangelical in the church. In fact, most Christians, even most seminary students and ministers, do *not* have an adequate understanding of the key labels in the conflict, not even the label with which they most identify. Few know the history of these ideas and how the corresponding words first became precious before they were drafted for ideological infighting. They don't appreciate the sociological principles that explain the conflict. They don't grasp the theological insights that guide a meaningful resolution. They understand neither the demanding countercultural nature of the solution nor why moderates have the most natural and least compromised access to this solution.

Avoidance of inflammatory words and inventing new names for old viewpoints are half measures at best. There is no quick fix to the problem of cultural and ecclesiastical pluralism in all its sociological, theological, and spiritual depth. Dealing with it requires walking through the fires of painful words and bitter resentment. We must spiritually confront our own demonic hostility to the Other in all its forms. Christians should be inspired to do this by their own journey of discipleship. At some level, they know that following Jesus Christ makes homeless beggars of us all, gratefully serving the kingdom of God, committed to the reign of God and not to a fruitless ideological triumph.

We contend that "liberal" and "evangelical" really do belong together. The "and" that joins them is not sappy "can't we all just get along" hopefulness but a considered judgment about the historic meanings and inherent possibilities of the two ideas. Liberal and conservative are opposites, in many ways, but liberal and evangelical need not be, just as conservative and evangelical clearly are not at the present time. Many people already sense this is true but lack confidence and guidance. We will sometimes refer to such people as *liberal-evangelical* Christian moderates. This recalls a mostly forgotten designation that has been important in the past. We think it should become important once again. We will survey the history of the term "liberal-evangelical" and of the constituent words "liberal" and "evangelical" in Part V.

CHAPTER 5

Reasons for the Emergence of Liberal-Evangelical Christianity

There is not a uniquely important reason why discerning moderate Christians make the decision to transcend the liberal versus evangelical conflict and commit themselves to church unity in the face of theological and political diversity. Our numerous conversations and interviews lead us to conclude that there are at least four distinct reasons, each a tangle of negative and positive motivations. The negative reasons are reactions against the kinds of Christian faith and church life people have experienced. The positive reasons are deeply held convictions that don't easily find a home, except in what we are calling a liberal-evangelical faith setting.

We think these distinctions directly influence people's criteria for church-shopping expeditions, their feelings about their home churches, and their reasons for trying to be faithful Christians by staying away from church altogether. They express a multifaceted critique of animosity in the churches, polarization in politics, and our society's moral priorities. They have solid biblical and theological foundations. We believe it is crucial for moderate seminary students, working pastors, and lay church leaders to think about them carefully, and we think moderate Christians of all sorts will strongly identify with at least some of them.

FRUSTRATION MEETS LOVE

First, we have repeatedly heard people describe their frustration with political and religious polarization. These folk would not be frustrated if, like some of their friends, they could identify wholeheartedly with one of the opposing agendas, but they simply do not. Some know both sides well enough to feel drawn to both. Others know only one side but sense something is missing. Either way, discerning moderate Christians experience the frustration of not fitting in, of witnessing a fight that seems wrongheaded and self-destructive, of feeling overwhelmed by the situation and not knowing how to change it.

This frustration meets its match in a deep conviction among moderates that God's love is more important than doctrinal or political unanimity. Moderate Christians feel intuitively certain it ought to be possible to find a home worshiping and serving alongside good-hearted political and theological opponents. They are inspired by a principled vision of Christian unity, grounded in the way Jesus united different people in his ministry and driven by the belief that all human distinctions fall away before the God who creates and judges us. It is the vision of a longed-for home that replaces frustration with a creative challenge: to forge meaningful identity through shared worship and social action in an inclusive community.

FEAR MEETS HOPE

Second, we often noticed fear among those we talked to: fear of cultural conflicts that constantly threaten to break into violence, fear of the global effects of a shortsighted empire mentality within the United States, fear of the death of authentic Christianity, fear of reducing Christianity to a political tool for rationalizing the social visions of left and right, and fear of fundamentalists who think nothing of neglecting this world or deliberately praying and working for the end of the world because they are so certain there is a better world to come.

These fears seem to find their answer in tireless hope: hope that tolerance and cooperation can defeat dangerous religious and political extremism, hope that a Christ-centered church that prioritizes radical inclusiveness can increase national and global compassion and understanding, hope that the church can set an example of love and forgiveness that changes lives. Hope often enough is a mere substitute for a real solution, an understandable escape from the harsh realities of desperate situations. But in this case, hope seems realistically grounded in the long history of human civilization, in which love and goodness and wisdom repeatedly wrestle down hatred and evil and stupidity, at least for a while. Discerning moderates see these as powerful fruits of the Spirit of God fueled by communities at worship, struggling saints at prayer, and compassion that drives human beings to help one another again and again.

DISMAY MEETS GRATITUDE

Third, we believe dismay, in the double sense of discouragement and alarm, is an important reason people seek a liberal-evangelical form of moderate Christianity. We have heard many moderates express dismay about the way Jesus Christ has no real role in the worship and spirituality and teaching of their churches; it is as if people do not know what to do with Jesus or are embarrassed by him. In other cases, dismay arises because the image of Christ is distorted to fit the ideological bias of the congregation or the personality of the preacher. We also hear dismay over the way churches approach the Bible: dismay at biblical illiteracy on the one side and dismay at the abuse of the Bible as an encyclopedia of proof texts on the other side. We hear dismay over churches that treat discipleship either as a merely optional lifestyle preference or as a psychologically coercive mirroring of the church leadership's beliefs and actions. People have spoken to us particularly of their dismay over the loss of Christian moral integrity, which has made Christians a cultural joke. Some Christians fight with each other to the point of rabid hatred over details that are

unintelligible to those outside the church, people Christians supposedly seek to influence morally and spiritually. They see some
Christians displaying a perverse form of self-righteousness and
judgmental hypocrisy, while others don't take their own faith
seriously enough to identify a clearly communicable stand on
key moral issues. They are dismayed by the psychological inno-
cence of Christians who pronounce convenient rationalizations
for hatred and bigotry, as in "love the sinner but hate the sin"
or "the Bible says it and that settles it." They find it difficult to
take Christians seriously when they don't participate in church
programs as a staple of life.

Yet spiritually lively, moderate Christians also bear a profound gratitude for life in the ambit of divine love, for a church
that cares, for the opportunities to grow in faith and to learn
compassion and courage in the face of life's challenges. They are
humbly grateful that they do not have to remain trapped in their
sins and that they have a chance to follow Jesus Christ and de-
vote themselves to the Christian Way. They feel it is impossible
to remain bogged down in the discouragement and disappointment of dismay when they are buoyed up by gratitude. Most
dismayed moderate Christians do not give up on the church but,
out of profound gratitude, seem to deepen their resolve. Those
who do give up on the organized church make a strong effort
to build less formal communities of Christian worship and service through which to express their gratitude for divine love and
grace.

Disgust Meets Wisdom

Fourth, we frequently hear reports of disgust. Disgust is a state
of mind that begins with spontaneous repulsion in reaction to
something we see or hear or feel or taste or imagine. It is the
"yuck factor," a trigger for fabulous facial contortions and over-
powering visceral feelings. From these primal sensory roots it
leads to action: we avoid what disgusts us or we attack it with
fury born of aversion. It is a potent force in forming moral convictions because we readily associate what disgusts us with moral

impurity. We have heard moderate Christians express their disgust particularly in reaction to the self-righteousness of Christian infighting, the arrogance of doctrinal and moral absolutism, and the brutal inconsistency of judgmental exclusion by people who are themselves sinners before God and unable to love their political and religious enemies. Moderates are disgusted by famous televangelists making judgmental pronouncements about how others should live while covertly and, in some cases, bizarrely betraying their own marriage vows. They are disgusted by ignorant left-wing attacks on conservative moral critiques of American society and by unfair public caricatures of conservatives as embarrassing anti-intellectual reactionaries, as if the moral tone of society did not need to be maintained and lifted.

Discerning moderates typically realize that it takes wisdom to make sense of our instinctively aggressive reaction to that which disgusts us. They tend to think carefully about what to do rather than rushing to a knee-jerk equation of the disgusting with the evil. It is possible to be disgusted by certain foods but then learn to overcome disgust in the presence of good people who eat them. That happened to one of us in the far north of China, eating dog soup for breakfast on a painfully cold morning with generous and kind hosts, and again in Belgium eating gourmet snails with wonderful companions. The very idea of these foods was viscerally disgusting, but good people eat them all the time so these feelings of disgust reflect upbringing and dietary habits more than the poor judgment of those who eat them regularly. This shows that we should hesitate to equate things that disgust us with impurity and evil.

A good example is well-known evangelist and sociologist Tony Campolo, who believes wisdom is taking a backseat to disgust on the homosexuality issue in the churches. He believes the Bible outlaws homosexual acts but also insists on the reliability of his research, which leads him to conclude that very few people choose their sexual orientation and few are ever able to change it (those who do appear to change probably make a different selection of life options rather than actually altering their orientation). Thus, he is appalled by the disgust-driven lack of acceptance of homosexual people in many churches. To him, this refusal to extend the hand of fellowship and support shows that the church lacks wisdom and is blindly enslaved by disgust.

Campolo is a good model for discerning moderate Christians. Though certain aspects of the Christian church cause them frustration, fear, dismay, and disgust, they refuse to give up on it. Rather, they cultivate the virtues of love, hope, gratitude, and wisdom, and allow these to prevail over their impulses to avoid or attack the object of their discomfort. They stay engaged, always looking for a way to make a positive difference.

A Moderate Conclusion

If you are a moderate Christian of the liberal-evangelical type, how might Part II's analysis of polarized rhetoric and demographics affect your self-understanding? What can you do, practically and positively, about this new self-understanding?

First, regarding self-understanding, we believe that *moderate Christians will be encouraged to discover they have a lot of company in the messy middle*. Indeed, you are a part of a resurgence of moderate Christians who are resisting the misplaced enthusiasms of political and religious extremes. You will probably be relieved to hear that someone is saying what you have been trying to say yourself.

There are moderate Christians of the liberal-evangelical type in every church in our country. Most don't know they have a name. They may not know they have company in their beliefs. They probably don't suspect that their radically inclusive, Christ-centered faith represents a ray of hope for American Christianity in the future. But they are everywhere. Some fortunate congregations have large numbers of them, which leads to fascinating corporate experiments in radical inclusiveness.

One of us recalls a council meeting at one such liberal-evangelical church. The pastor announced to his leadership team that he was going to a conference to speak to and spend time with a group of liberal and evangelical pastors. The council secretary let out an uncharacteristic laugh that drew the attention of the other council members. She quickly apologized for her outburst and then said, "You mean there are other people like us?" Yes. That is exactly what we mean. Liberal and evangelical not only *can* go together, liberal and evangelical *are* together in individual people of faith and in certain communities, and we believe that is where some of the most exciting faith movement is occurring.

Second, regarding action, if you are a moderate Christian with a dawning sense that a breakthrough in self-understanding might be possible for you, then *the practical and positive next step is to invest time and effort in learning about the profoundly counter-cultural center of Christianity*. The demographics show that you belong to a large and diverse group, it is true, but that doesn't mean you have nothing in common with your fellow moderates. There are patterns among your viewpoints, good reasons for your resistance to extremes, and an identifiable history that you can learn to claim as your distinctive heritage.

Unfortunately, the swollen ranks of moderate Christians have rarely been called upon to think out who they are and to lift their voices on behalf of the Christ-centered radical inclusiveness they prize. Most moderates we have met are frustrated that the Christian movement seems to be enslaved to cultural polarization rather than setting an example of unity that reflects the radically inclusive love it proclaims. They often feel neglected, longing for guidance and inspiration suited to their moderate mindset. They sometimes feel anxious about church unity. Feeling lost in the middle of a culturally, politically, and religiously polarized context can be profoundly disabling.

Yet these same moderates are more committed to their faith than ever, and passionate about its social and spiritual relevance. Just knowing the demographics can give moderates the boost in confidence they need to invest energy in deepening their self-understanding. A small amount of well-earned encouragement can inspire them to fight for a clear vision of a way forward as Christian disciples within churches proclaiming a message of radical inclusiveness. But, like education in every domain of life, there are no shortcuts here. The issues are complex and understanding is hard-won.

You can use this book to guide your educational efforts. Find a group of friends to read it with you, at whatever pace suits you.

We recommend one chapter each week in a group setting. Use the study guides on LiberalEvangelical.org to go deeper into the demographic issues of Part II, the political issues raised in Part III, the sociological analyses of Part IV, and the historical material in Part V. Because we are talking about action that creates a change in self-understanding, consider keeping a diary of your thoughts. When you are finished, read back over what you have written to see how far you have come.

PART III

A Cultural Divide in American Christianity

CHAPTER 6

The Liberal-Conservative Split in Politics

POLITICAL LABELS AND THE MUDDY MIDDLE

Barely a day goes by without some comment on the conflict between liberals and conservatives within contemporary U.S. politics. The theme floods op-ed pieces and pundit conversations, television and radio, newspaper editorials and internet blogs, talk shows and news outlets. An enormous number of books on the subject plumb the depths from economic, moral, and religious points of view—usually with a populist, polarized tone. Ironically, this saturation of information constructs as much as describes the conflict. Despite all this chatter, most Americans remain, as always, within an easy stroll from the political middle. Voter polls and close election results give ample evidence of the dominance of moderates, as do the survey data we presented in Part I.

Time and again we have met self-described moderate conservatives and self-described moderate liberals who seem to agree on just about everything. They don't want to persecute gays, but they don't want to weaken the family-based fabric of society. They don't want to force women into back alleys in search of abortions, but they are horrified by the frequency of abortion and particularly appalled by convenience abortions. They want government to care for the defenseless, but they don't want people to abuse tax-based handouts. They want a small and efficient government, but they also want corporate regulation because they don't trust the profit motive to regulate itself. They want religious ideals to influence politics, but they don't want the two domains merged. They want a vigorous national defense, but they do not like being misled by the government about reasons for war and they hate to see their armed forces in harm's way. They want vigorous international trade but do not want factory and farmworkers to be forced out of work.

Morris Florina's *Culture War?* effectively lays out the case for the dominance of moderates in American politics and criticizes exaggerated claims about a culture war in politics and morals. There is polarization in U.S. politics, and it does have heavy moral and religious overtones, but most Americans are close to the political and moral middle no matter where in the country they live. It is the loud voices of the left and right, as amplified by competing media outlets, that produce the impression of a massive culture war. There is a culture war, but it is much less strongly correlated with U.S. geography than most Americans realize, and it is unconvincing to the magnificent moderate majority.

With so much in common, why do moderates of all political persuasions label themselves in opposite ways? People describe themselves based on the way words are used in their local subculture. The words "liberal" and "conservative" carry overtones that evoke powerful—but different—feelings depending on where you live and who your friends and family are. Some overtones are deeply attractive, as when "liberal" suggests freedom from tyranny and the privilege of making up your own mind, and "conservative" suggests the preservation of hearth and home and the traditions that make us feel warm and safe.

Other overtones are repellent, especially in relation to the extremes of the opposite side. When some Americans call themselves liberal, it may be partly because they find far-right conservatives appalling—as in "those damned conservatives are bigoted warmongers," inspired by conservatives such as Pat Robertson, with his outrageous call for the United States to assassinate the democratically elected leader of Venezuela or his blatant insulting of Muslims or his saying that only Christians and Jews should hold political office in the United States. When some Americans call themselves conservative, it may be partly because they find far-left liberals morally repellent—as in "those damned liberals are godforsaken perverts," inspired by the American Civil Liberties Union's defense of live sex shows (*State of Oregon v. Ciancanelli*, 2005; *City of Nyssa v. Dufloth/Smith*, 2005) and child pornography (*People v. Ferber*, 1981, later overturned by the Supreme Court). Feeling repelled by one extreme is often enough to push a moderate to adopt the label of the opposite camp, whatever it may be. These contextual and emotional factors mean that political labels can mislead. They can cause us to forget about the vast messy middle where there is strong agreement over most important issues, where most people try to be good to their neighbors and kind to strangers, where upright citizens care about communities and prize virtues of honesty and integrity.

We think much the same is true of the religious version of the liberal-conservative division within American Christianity. The relevant factors are vague words, local ways of speaking, strong feelings of attraction and aversion, focusing on the extremes, and ignoring the complicated middle. The liberal-conservative cultural divide fuels the tension between liberals and evangelicals within our churches. We need to understand the politics enough to grasp its religious influence and, in turn, how religion influences politics.

THE SOCIOLOGY OF POLITICAL FIGHTS

The conflict between liberal and conservative political elements in the United States has a complex history reaching back to the immigrant founding of the new nation. This story is fascinating, and many historians have written about it. We offer here not another sketch but rather an answer to a series of key questions about the emergence of this political conflict—questions that are important for understanding our current situation. What is at stake in the tension between liberals and conservatives? What does each side care most deeply about? On what basis can we find sympathy with our political enemies? Above all, why are we fighting?

Let's face it: all societies fight, all communities fight, all families fight, and all friends fight. Some of the fights are obvious, others are masked by superficial courtesy; some are violent, others wordy; some are short-lived explosions of frustration, others are perpetually simmering feuds. Most fighting is partially self-destructive, but that does not stop us. Fighting is not the only thing we do, and it is not our most inspiring pastime, but it *is* a basic part of the human condition.

Our needs in small groups such as friends and families are mostly psychological and spiritual. We count on a larger society for services and safety, civilization and culture. We don't ask our spouse to solve the problem of a military attack by a hostile nation, and we don't expect the state to heal our sin-sick souls. But the principle is the same at all levels: we fight for what we need and believe. We fight with those who we think can provide what we need and with those who stand in our way of getting it. We fight on behalf of those we care about as well as ourselves. If we weren't in a liberal versus conservative fight, then we would be fighting over something else.

Fighting is significantly a group phenomenon. People are complicated to start with, but groups of them evolve into extremely complex institutions, with many unintended side effects. Human life is difficult to control at the best of times, even with mostly functional institutions to help keep us organized. We only need to ponder countries lacking stable institutions to realize how precious they are, and yet we only need to look at the way our own society's institutions work to realize how vulnerable to decay they can be. That's why institutions, once imaginatively created, need to be protected and corrected as long as they remain valuable. Most people realize this, and so they are willing to spend a lot of time and energy fighting over these precious and vital institutions.

Reinhold Niebuhr, one of our liberal-evangelical heroes, made a powerful argument about institutional side effects in his famous book, *Moral Man and Immoral Society*. As the title suggests, he thought most human problems worth fighting over emerge at the social level. He argued that only good-hearted people, including people of faith, can properly contain the inevitable, unplanned ill effects of social arrangements. Niebuhr might have been a bit one-sided in his analysis. His brother H. Richard Niebuhr quipped that it would be just as true to say that individual human beings are the fount of immorality and that society is a civilizing force that promotes morality. But we know what Reinhold was saying. Someone is always on the wrong side of every business decision, every communal consensus, and every political platform.

The explanation for liberal-conservative fighting does not lie in the sheer fact of it, as if we could just stop by putting our minds to it, like children fighting over toys. Rather, the explanation lies in substantive ideological differences about how to protect and reform the institutions we rely upon for civilization and culture, safety and security, health and well-being. There are strategic differences between liberals and conservatives that cannot be eliminated because they reflect major options in organizing human societies. Just as the two Niebuhr brothers disagreed authentically, and just as every ancient political tradition has debated the same problem, so liberals and conservatives will disagree. There really is something to fight over here. The fight is important even though the optimal approach probably involves coordinating wisdom from both sides.

Many religious people think of the prominent liberal-conservative tension in the United States exclusively in terms of theology or morality. They take the civilizational and institutional aspects of their lives for granted, except when it comes time to lobby for something in particular, such as a presidential candidate or a Supreme Court appointment. The liberal-conservative tension in politics is obviously related to values and beliefs. But there is much more. Two of the differences between political liberals and conservatives directly involve the roles institutions play in our corporate life: *institutional expectations* and *church-state relations*. A third difference between liberals and conservatives has to do with different *styles of moral reasoning*. Together, these three considerations help to explain both liberal-conservative fighting in politics and its influence on the liberal-conservative divide within Christianity. We will discuss these three themes here and in the succeeding two chapters.

LIBERALS VERSUS CONSERVATIVES
ON INSTITUTIONAL ROLES

Our social reality is created, not just received. Vast institutions did not exist at one point, and now they do. The creation of our society reflects the values and ideals of its founders and, subsequently, of those who nurtured and reformed it. Our society is conditioned by memories of the persecution the pilgrims fled, their struggles to survive in a new country, and by the dreams of early immigrant Americans. All of these early Americans imagined social institutions as ways for them and their descendants to get what we need with a minimum of anxiety and fighting. Thus, our received social reality carries forward very old disputes about whether institutions should provide for particular needs in the lives of Americans and, if so, which ones.

For example, most of us want to feel comfortable with the morals expressed in our society. This is one of our deepest needs, so different moral opinions soon lead us to fight over "values." We may feel despair because of the unanticipated failure of our social institutions to sustain the moral virtues we prize. But we are also inspired by the hope that renewing key institutions can improve moral tone.

These battles sometimes involve efforts to control or influence other people's behavior, which provokes indignation and resentment and gives the impression that the fight is mostly between people who disagree on particular values and are morally judgmental toward one another. But this is a misleading impression. In fact, the vast majority of liberals and conservatives fundamentally agree on basic values that define the social fabric of civil life, such as courtesy, compassion, diligence, honesty, modesty, loyalty, and justice. They jointly resist the flouting of such values in the wider society.

Battle lines over abortion, gay marriage, and capital punishment seem to line up with the liberal-conservative divide in politics, but this is misleading, too. Liberal and conservative voting patterns on these issues have more to do with powerful convictions about the role the state should play in regulating personal life than with the moral values themselves. Contrary to the rhetoric of the "religious right" and the "loony left," there is no convincing way to divide the moral marbles between liberals and conservatives. We cannot effectively understand the liberal-conservative religious divide in terms of value issues alone.

Consider the Terri Schiavo case, which became political and religious dynamite toward the end of her tragic life on March 31, 2005. Terri was severely brain damaged in 1990 when she was twenty-six years old from a cardiac arrest, probably induced by her eating disorder. After a few months in a coma, she remained in a persistent vegetative state. She left no written instructions about her desired medical treatment in case she should ever be in such a condition. Her parents, Robert and Mary Schindler, disputed the diagnosis and fought her husband, Michael Shiavo, in and out of the courts for years over whether to remove Terri's feeding tube. We think most moderate liberals and moderate conservatives saw eye to eye on the moral issues in this case: it is very complicated, very tragic, and very personal; there is no single solution that will satisfy everyone; passionate opinions on all sides should be expressed openly and respectfully; and, if the matter cannot be resolved by individual conscience and negotiation between the interested parties, the dispute should be handled in the courts.

There was a significant gap between this moderate consensus and religious conservatives. For example, conservative Roman Catholics gathered around Pope John Paul II's statement that respect for life demands that nourishment be provided to people in persistent vegetative states, even when there is no hope for recovery. But a serious gap between political liberals and political conservatives only emerged over the question of government interference in the situation. Political conservatives tolerated or welcomed the Florida legislature's October 2003 intervention ("Terri's Law"), the attempt at U.S. congressional hearings, and Congress's attempt to overturn Florida's legal process with the "Palm Sunday Compromise." This was acceptable to strong conservatives because they expect their political institutions to be directly involved in upholding the moral values they prize.

Meanwhile, political liberals and many moderate conservatives were appalled by the governmental interference, regardless of their views on the moral questions, because they believe the state should leave such matters to individual conscience and, in cases of conflict, to the courts. The government would only be entitled to intervene in the legal process if there was overwhelming evidence of blatant criminal corruption, and then the intervention should be restrained and minimal.

This story illustrates the deeper fight between liberals and conservatives in the political arena. *This fight is not over morals only but also and perhaps primarily about institutional expectations.* People have very different expectations for who should fulfill their need to feel comfortable with the moral values expressed in society. Should the state regulate moral values or leave questions of moral values to individuals? What is the role of religious institutions in forming values and policing behavior? What are the roles of the courts, the schools, the police, families, corporations, and local communities?

In addition to different institutional expectations, people strongly disagree over appropriate strategies for getting what they want. Should we rely on the economy to produce opportunities for enjoyable lifestyles that invite people to embrace moral values such as thriftiness and community-mindedness, as in President Reagan's "trickle-down" economic theory? Should we resort to mass demonstrations to draw attention to injustice and moral failure, as in the civil rights movement and the Vietnam War protests? Should we work through the existing political system to produce desirable legislation as the religious right has done so effectively in recent decades? Should we take our fights to the courts as with *Roe v. Wade?* Should we use lethal force as in the murders of abortion clinic workers and the Oklahoma City bombing?

These strategic variations have religious translations. Should religious institutions limit themselves to inspiring moral behavior or lobby in the political arena for favorable legislation and regulation? Should they invest in mass-market mail and phone campaigns to raise consciousness or promote their moral values through patient example? Should they speak out on how to vote or leave political matters to the individual conscience? Should they sermonize on hot-button political and moral issues or focus on salvation and worship?

WHAT LIBERALS AND CONSERVATIVES ARE TRYING TO PROTECT

It is in relation to institutional expectations and strategies that we find the strongest correlations with liberals and conservatives.

Traditionally, liberals have stood for freedom, as the name suggests, and especially for freedom of the mind through education and freedom of the individual from political tyranny and religious control. Liberals want the freedom to speak what they believe to be true and to live according to their conscience. They expect the state to guarantee that basic right first and foremost by staying out of their lives and then by protecting democratic processes that allow angry voters to throw their political representatives out of office. But they also want a certain amount of state interference so long as it is according to liberal values. For example, just as they want the state to stay out of the mind-control, belief-control, and bedroom-control business, so they want the state to restrain other institutions that attempt to interfere with freedom—including religious institutions.

Liberals expect all kinds of institutions to make an effort to tolerate those with unexpected or unpopular opinions, including flag-burning Americans critical of the very government whose tolerance they depend on for their right to protest safely. They expect the state to nurture and defend a free press, even if it means interfering in the business world by regulating corporate control of the media. They expect the state to maintain the wall of separation between itself and religion, even if it means sometimes interfering in the affairs of local communities that see no harm in placing a statue of the Ten Commandments on prominent display outside a courthouse. They expect the state to defend the rights to freedom of the disenfranchised and oppressed because modern liberalism holds that freedom is every American's and every human being's birthright, regardless of race or sex or creed. They have high expectations for educational institutions at all levels and expect the state to support the goal of an educated and independently minded public, even if it means regulating public school curricula. They also expect the state to protect and care for those whose potential freedom is not fully realized, perhaps because of poverty or misfortune, even if it involves increasing taxes on the general population to pay for social welfare programs and subsidized health care. They want markets to be free for imaginative economic innovation, but they also expect the business world to promote freedom of information by telling the truth about products. They will accept governmental regulation to force truth telling when the profit motive overwhelms good citizenship in the corporate boardroom, and they defend the possibility of lawsuits to encourage business not to victimize consumers with negligent and dangerous products.

The general trend here is that liberals have more confidence in the *enlightened individual* than they do in political, economic, and social institutions. They do not trust vast political institutions to care for the suffering and marginalized, nor to protect individual freedoms, but they know they need those institutions to survive, so they take pains to build in safeguards and means of correction when institutions inevitably go astray. They rarely hesitate to change institutions if circumstances dictate. The social world of the liberal ideal is somewhat chaotic, a blessed quest for goodness and truth and beauty among the glorious savagery of nature and typical heartlessness of institutional machinery. Such an environment is not intrinsically morally structured as much as it is a perpetual opportunity for the discovery of moral bearings and the artful construction of the good life.

Conservatives have a contrasting set of expectations about which institutions should meet which of their vital needs. Traditionally, as the name suggests, conservatives have stood for the conservation of institutions and the preservation of the wisdom and values they encode. The general trend in this case is the opposite of liberalism: conservatives have more confidence in the *gyroscopic guidance of traditional institutions* than they do in individuals, even enlightened individuals, with their idiosyncratic opinions and chaotic behavior. They tend to honor the wisdom and values handed down over generations above the creative but often self-deceptive rationalizations of clever human beings. They do not trust individuals to agree spontaneously, and so they deem functional political, economic, and social institutions to be hard-won, precious, and in need of vigilant protection from the naive attacks of idealistic critics.

How do these general trends translate into concrete institutional expectations for conservatives? Conservatives expect first and foremost that their institutions at every level and in every domain of society will live up to the honor and respect bestowed upon them by people who submit to their authority. Thus, the character of politicians, executives, judges, and religious leaders matters as much as their performance. They expect the federal government to exercise political authority befitting its dignity and role and the church to exercise moral and spiritual authority proper to its important place in American life. Conservatives share the general U.S. disdain for political interference in religion, and the anxiety about totalitarianism, so they expect the federal government will confine its activities as much as possible only to those tasks that cannot be handled by other institutions. This includes especially international trade and diplomacy, basic services from transportation to national parks, and national defense. But when things go awry in one part of society, they count on government to intervene decisively, meting out just punishments as needed and curtailing civil rights for the sake of national security and moral integrity, if necessary.

Meanwhile, conservatives typically expect state governments to take up the space created by a properly contracted federal government and to enjoy significant authority in their own domains so as to allow for variations among the legal, political, and cultural traditions. State governments should restrain themselves so as to nurture the community-defining roles of local governments and social institutions. Religious institutions with a clear mandate to care for the poor should provide social services for those who drop out of mainstream economic and social life. The federal government should not attempt to do this because it lies outside its proper mandate. Responsibility for social health can be discharged less invasively and more efficiently by directing funds to the states and to on-the-ground institutions such as faith-based organizations that carry out caring activities. For their part, corporate leaders should set a moral example appropriate to the power they wield. They should regulate themselves in light of universal moral standards of fairness, honesty, and social responsibility. But they should also enjoy the financial and lifestyle benefits derived from their initiative and diligence. The social world of the conservative ideal is above all consistent and intelligible, with rewards and punishments fitted to a scale of moral goods. Every institution and individual has a role in a well-ordered, morally structured scheme.

The particular hot-button issues that define the political tension between liberals and conservatives vary. One year it is whether to go or remain at war, another it is whether the federal government should fund the social work of religious institutions, and yet another it is whether governments or local institutions and religious groups are better suited to oversee the education of children. This variation in hot-button issues can produce apparently contradictory policies, as when conservatives affirm the sanctity of constitutional documents in one era and seek a constitutional amendment banning gay marriage or flag burning in another, or when liberals stress education and self-determination in one decade and hefty social welfare in another. Yet the deeper contrasting intuitions about the roles of individuals and institutions in a healthy society have real staying power and outlast the passing trends. They reach far deeper into the practical meaning of liberalism and conservatism in politics.

THE BROAD SYMPATHIES OF POLITICAL MODERATES

When liberal and conservative intuitions are stated in this way, we believe most people have some affinity for both sides, even if they lean to one side or the other on particular hot-button issues. That's why moderates are such a large group.

The political moderate is one who feels skeptical *both* about the ability of individuals to regulate the unanticipated side effects of institutions *and* about the capacity of institutions to cultivate morally responsible individuals. Put positively, they have *limited confidence* in both individuals and institutions. Strict liberals lean consistently one way in relation to this contrast, while strict conservatives lean consistently the opposite way. But moderates assert the importance of a dynamic give-and-take between institutions and individuals. In any given case, they look to see what has gone wrong and press on the individual or on the institutional side more strongly as a result.

This is what can give the appearance of inconsistency to the incautious observer, especially when compared with the simple consistencies of the right and the left. In fact, the moderate approach can be an utterly consistent implementation of the deeper principle that individuals and institutions must dynamically adjust to one another to achieve the virtues of civilization and a richly expressive culture. *Moderates often feel lost in the middle, but there is a way of talking about their centrist location that is positive, clear, and attractive.*

As a crystallizing example, consider the abortion debate in the United States. For liberals, an abortion decision should be a personal matter, as with most moral and body-related issues. Government should stay out of it, and the courts should limit themselves to fending off legislative interference and handling any disputes that may arise. Government should not tie foreign aid to restrictions on acceptable birth control advice or withhold funds from groups that advocate the use of condoms as one way to prevent the spread of HIV/AIDS. Liberals will stick to this view even when they are appalled by the frequency of abortion and pray and work for a change in worldwide moral conscience, from the behaviors that produce unwanted pregnancies to the use of rape as a weapon of war. The *Roe v. Wade* decision is one that helps to define abortion as a personal moral and body-related decision for women, a decision to be made with the advice of doctors and other involved parties.

For conservatives, by contrast, it is the duty of the government to insert itself into this issue despite its personal, bodily character because something has gone morally haywire. Governments should pass legislation to limit or ban abortion, it should appoint Supreme Court justices who will overturn or chip away at the *Roe v. Wade* ruling, it should support close access of anti-abortion protestors to abortion clinics, and it should restrict foreign aid based on whether potential recipients support its views of reproductive ethics, regardless of cultural or religious differences.

The moral issues surrounding abortion matter a great deal, of course, but they are not reliable indicators of voting patterns among moderates. Expectations for political and social institutions matter more. Most political moderates tend to agree on the moral issues: typically, they want abortion to be safe, legal, and rare, and they want to protect rape victims from having to carry a child conceived in a violent attack. But moderates have an even clearer consensus on institutional roles in the abortion debate: government should not legislate over the bodies of women, and other institutions should encourage pregnant women to exercise responsibility both toward other people involved in their decision and toward the growing life within them. This consensus about institutional roles and personal responsibility most influences the way moderates vote.

Our fundamental intuitions about the roles of institutions have powered the liberal-conservative tension in politics for a long time and continue to do so today—beneath and behind the more prominent controversies that hit the news.

CHAPTER 7

Relations between Religion and Society

We have described the familiar fact that human beings fight individually and in groups of all sizes for what they need, want, or believe. We have said that the liberal-conservative tension in politics is born in disagreements about strategies for getting what we need and expectations about who or what should provide for our needs. So the next question concerns the two-way influence between religion and this political tension.

THE ROLE OF RELIGION IN PROTECTING DEMOCRACY

The perennial and universal political problems are stability and flexibility. The best societies organize and protect themselves so that they can remain relatively stable, thereby permitting economic and cultural activities to flourish. They also respond quickly and effectively to changing circumstances, minimizing stress and disruption. Behind these practical problems lie questions about the values that a society should manifest, such as justice, peace, and personal self-expression. In front of these problems lie questions about the optimal political system for achieving a stable and flexible embodiment of prized values. At one point in the development of human civilizations, a lack of education and widespread illiteracy made democracy an impractical ideal. In our time, however, democracy is a messy but practical political system. As the old saying goes, expressed in various forms by James Madison, Winston Churchill, and others, democracy might not be perfect, but it is the least imperfect system we know. The vast majority of U.S. citizens prize their democratic system of government as a hard-won set of institutions and laws with fabulous benefits for society and individuals.

When a basically sound political system is already in place, it is natural to worry. What dangers does democracy face? What social developments threaten its ability to function optimally? Can we recognize looming threats? These questions have concerned political theorists since the birth of modern democratic nation-states. Two of the deepest insights into the viability of American democracy are quite old.

First, British historian Edward Gibbon gave an analysis of a great political disaster in the six volumes of *The History of the Decline and Fall of the Roman Empire*, written between 1774 and 1788. Gibbon's account is long and detailed, but he does suggest that the slow political and military decline of Rome was the result of an internal moral decay. Gibbon held strong Enlightenment values concerning the responsibility of politicians and the freedom of individual citizens, which no doubt helped to produce this conclusion. He did not know about the effects, including irreversible brain damage, of lead poisoning from the Roman water system, and his understanding of economic factors was not as comprehensive as in recent analyses. His insight is fundamental for political and social life, however, and it applies to liberal democracies such as the United States as well as to the ancient political accomplishment of Rome.

Today, conservatives commonly express anxiety over the collapse of the American dream based on the moral decay of society. It is for the sake of the preservation of the American ideal that conservatives tolerate morality-based limits on personal freedom and security-based limits on civil rights. They fear a foolish idealism that would assert individual liberty so strongly as to endanger the foundations of American society. Liberals have the opposite fear. They fight incursions into what they take to be the real genius of American society, namely, its principled elevation of personal liberty, with associated freedoms of speech and opinion and religion. They fervently believe that, without genuine liberty, American civilization will not be worth protecting. Both wings of American politics clearly register Gibbon's warning about moral decay but in ways that suit their characteristic patterns of institutional expectation.

Second, French sociologist Alexis de Tocqueville gave a famous analysis of American democracy in the two volumes of *Democracy in America*, published in 1835 to 1840. Tocqueville based the book on his 1831 tour investigating the prison system of the United States, but the book covers virtually every aspect of American democracy. He noted the peculiar pragmatism of American democracy, the mixed blessing of a free press, and the dangers of materialist consumerism—observations that ring true today. One of his shrewdest predictions was that American democracy would tend to stay healthy so long as the American people participated in *voluntary associations that both exercised public influence and offered moral orientation*—and he had churches in mind, especially.

Tocqueville reasoned as follows. Voluntary associations that define and nurture moral values create resistance to governmental and corporate corruption, forge a strong sense of moral orientation and social responsibility in individuals, and serve as locations for political debate and dissemination of political ideas. When people voluntarily participate in such groups, they activate these democracy-preserving virtues. When voluntary associations lose willing participants or political influence, these advantages vanish, and American democracy becomes vulnerable to corruption, then demagoguery, and eventually totalitarianism.

We think we detect some idealism in Tocqueville's analysis, and we can think of instances of demagoguery that seem to go hand in glove with voluntary associations, such as McCarthyism. But there is a deep insight in Tocqueville's reading of the importance of churches and similar groups to the health of American democracy. That insight holds good even in our very different situation almost two centuries later. Some in the extreme religious right may continue to nurture the political ideal of a theocracy under a godly leader but moderate conservatives are content to activate the virtues Tocqueville described by making sure religious groups are strong and have a healthy political voice. Moderate liberals also acknowledge Tocqueville's wisdom. In keeping with their skepticism about monochromatic institutional monopolies and their emphasis on civil rights, liberals work to ensure that a wide variety of religious groups and other voluntary associations have a voice.

Wuthnow's Orange

One of the best accounts of the politics-religion issue in the United States is sociologist Robert Wuthnow's *The Struggle for America's Soul: Evangelicals, Liberals, and Secularism.* Wuthnow traces the liberal-conservative conflict through its early roots up to the mid-1980s. He distinguishes three sectors of American society in a highly generalized but thought-provoking way. The *state* is the locus of political and military power, the administrators and protectors of society. The *marketplace* is the locus of economic activity that provides goods and services in return for a profit. The *voluntary* sector is, in the first instance, everything else. It is the spontaneous formation of groups with common interests. Some of these groups give people leverage in the marketplace, such as consumer interest groups. Some confer political power and facilitate discussion of vital social issues, such as the American Civil Liberties Union or the Christian Coalition or the League of Women Voters. Others have no economic or political motive but exist simply because people want to do things together, such as play tennis or worship God. The voluntary sector is private in respect to not being subject to direct state management or economic influence. Yet it is also potentially public in respect to the way voluntary groups can amass political and economic influence. Wuthnow's third sector corresponds, roughly, to Tocqueville's voluntary associations.

Wuthnow likens the three sectors to segments of an orange. One large wedge of segments is the state and another is the marketplace. A smaller wedge of segments interfaces with both large wedges, suggesting the role the voluntary sector plays in mediating and monitoring and motivating political and economic activity. He locates private activity close to the center of the orange and public activity close to the outer edge, thereby rightly indicating that politics and economics have both public and private dimensions, despite being essentially public phenomena. It is at the boundaries between the third sector and both the state and market sectors that religion is affected by and affects the surrounding culture.

Religious inspiration and influence occurs in much the way that the insights of Gibbon and Tocqueville suggest is essential. The marketplace and state cannot easily produce the moral resources they need to function effectively. But moral bearings are a renewable resource so long as people voluntarily associate with religious and other morality-nurturing groups and so long as such voluntary associations have the capacity to influence the state and the marketplace. When voluntary associations decline, it is as if Wuthnow's third sector of orange segments withers and contracts, causing the rest of the orange to rot.

Wuthnow expresses concern over the squeezing out of the third sector altogether, either through declining involvement in voluntary associations or because these voluntary associations lose their influence. This concern repeats and updates Tocqueville's view that third-sector activities, and especially religion, are crucial for political and social stability. It is not hard to see why Wuthnow would worry. Most people today can picture:

- a bureaucratized state making third-sector discussion irrelevant to politics,
- an economic juggernaut defined by a free market and material acquisitiveness that is immune to moderation or critique from the third sector,
- shrinking involvement that reduces the moral influence of religious groups,
- growing pluralism that weakens effective debate over social issues through a cacophony of conflicting perspectives, and
- religious groups losing their public credibility through internal conflicts and ideological extremism.

We see evidence of each of these dangerous trends in contemporary American church-society relations. But we also see countertrends aimed at preserving valuable social institutions and reforming them through third-sector reassertion. These countertrends include churches that are renewing their congregational life, regaining their moral influence, and striving for a public voice. In the United States, especially since Wuthnow's book was published in 1989, we see energized discussion of "religion in the public square" among Mainline Protestants, more pointed Vatican-supported social commentary among Catholics, and a more refined entrance into American politics from conservatives. As these dynamic movements unfold, Wuthnow's orange helps us remember that these patterns of mutual interdependence are extremely important for both U.S. society and churches.

Religious Influence on State and Marketplace

A large majority of Americans would probably accept Wuthnow's orange, or some variation of it, as a description of the way religious groups influence the political and marketplace sectors of U.S. society. But politics and religion in the United States and elsewhere are awash in fights over the best way to exercise this influence.

The Marketplace Sector

In relation to the marketplace sector, for example, it is easy to agree that we absolutely need honest corporate officers, especially after numerous high-profile disasters of corrupt corporate management involving Adelphia, Arthur Andersen, Enron, Merck, and WorldCom, among others. It is easy to stipulate that corporations should serve shareholders not only by trying to make a profit but also by acting in accordance with the simplest consensus moral values of those shareholders, not to mention the laws of the land. It is easy to see how executives voluntarily participating in a religious group could help to make corporate boardrooms more compassionate and responsible places. None of this is particularly controversial.

By contrast, it is very difficult to agree about how churches should express their views on corporate greed and corruption, on the acquisitiveness of Americans, or on the economic system itself. This is where the liberal-conservative political divide rears its head with markedly opposed visions of church influence. Should churches bestow their approval on a capitalist economy and the acquisitiveness that drives it? Should they treat material gain as a divine blessing, as so many megachurches and independent congregations do? Should they focus instead on material inequities and corporate exploitation of children and the poor? The moral logics here are quite opposed.

On the one hand, politically conservative church folk tend to see the capitalist marketplace as another God-given institution, like democracy and the church itself. They often represent material blessing as the divine reward of individual Christian faithfulness or of the United States' national righteousness as God's chosen nation. Over two decades of survey data bear this out. The 1987 Lilly Endowment's Church and Community Project showed that one-third of Americans believe that personal success is a sign of God's blessing, and that number rises to well over two-thirds among certain conservative religious groups. Likewise, the Pew Research Center's 2002 Religion and Public Life Survey shows that almost half of Americans believe that the United States has enjoyed special protection from God for most of its history. The 2006 Baylor Religion Survey found that almost one in five agreed with the even stronger assertion that God favors the United States in world affairs, with the large majority of these being politically conservative. Why shouldn't God's provision of institutional benefits extend to politics and economics and lifestyle? And why shouldn't churches urge their members to participate energetically in the economic opportunities before them and to enjoy the benefits that result, with thankfulness? This view postulates a harmonious and intimate connection between the marketplace segment and the third-sector of Wuthnow's orange at both the private (inner-orange) and public (outer-orange) levels.

On the other hand, the liberal suspicion of institutions and their unplanned negative side effects leads inevitably to tension between third-sector churches and the marketplace. Liberal churches tend not to think of the institutional status quo as a divine blessing. Rather, they judge the economy and marketplace based on its effects on the poor and the marginalized, the most vulnerable members of society, and in terms of their commitment to fairer distribution of wealth around the world. They tend to believe social justice is the biblical criterion of economic institutions.

The State Sector

In relation to the state sector, everyone agrees publicly that political leaders should resist the many opportunities for corruption and model the highest standards of honesty, compassion, intelligence, and courage. And most would grant that such virtues are not produced within the political system itself but need to be brought into the state sector from the outside for the sake of the nation's political health and effectiveness.

Despite these points of consensus, disagreement breaks out regularly about religion's role in influencing politics and politicians. Can we trust religious institutions to have an appropriate moral influence on politicians or do churches tend merely to produce narrow-minded ideologues? Should politicians wear their religious convictions on their sleeves, striving to implement legislation favored within their religious group? Can we trust politicians whose religious convictions lead them to critique economic conditions based solely on the existence of a poor underclass without ever taking seriously the importance of flourishing economies for stable social life?

Conservatives tend to value a more highly national identity, its articulation in military terms, and the ideal of sacrifice for the defense of national political ideals. Thus, conservative churches readily align themselves with patriotic impulses and consistently support military action with an eye to long-term survival of God-given American political institutions. In contrast, liberals tend toward suspicion of institutions in all things including military action and its various public rationales. Thus, liberal churches tend to foment protest against wars, drawing attention to hidden or mixed motives. They follow U.S. President Dwight Eisenhower in his famous 1961 farewell speech when he warned of collusion and misplaced power in the military-industrial complex: "We should take nothing for granted. Only an alert and knowledgeable citizenry can compel the proper meshing of the huge industrial and military machinery of defense with our peaceful methods and goals so that security and liberty may prosper together."

The Bible and Religious Influence on Political Views

There is a lot in the Bible about religion and politics. So it is not surprising that beliefs about the Bible are important factors in fights among Christians about religious influence on politics and economics. The 2006 Baylor Religion Survey confirms this and diagnoses what it is about religion that really makes the difference in political viewpoints.

On the surface there are significant correlations between religious denominations and standard measures of political conservatism. For example, the scores on the Political Conservatism Scale are significantly lower for Mainline Protestants (15.76) and Catholics (16.29) than for Evangelical Protestants (18.69). But this turns out to be misleading. The Baylor survey goes below the surface to discover that the biblical literalists in all three religious traditions score virtually the same on the Political Conservatism Scale (19.53, 19.88, and 20.11, respectively, with the differences statistically insignificant). It seems denominational differences in conservatism derive almost entirely from the number of biblical literalists in those denominations. *It is not denomination but religious attitude to the Bible that makes the difference.*

The Baylor study also showed that biblical literalists hold to conservative political agenda items and oppose liberal political agenda items far more strongly than any other demographic or faith-based grouping. Table 6 presents the summary, with the numbers representing correlations. Numbers close to 0 mean no correlation, +1 means complete positive correlation (total match), and -1 means complete negative correlation (total mismatch). The larger bold numbers indicate that the correlation is significant in the statistical framework of the study; other numbers are too close to zero. This is a complicated table but it rewards close study.

	Biblical Literalism	Religious Attendance	Evangelical Protestant	Mainline Protestant	Catholic
Conservative Agenda Items: Should the Government . . .					
Spend more on the military	**+.317**	**+.176**	**+.187**	-.005	+.027
Advocate Christian values	**+.508**	**+.450**	**+.349**	-.046	-.040
Punish criminals more harshly	**+.293**	**+.115**	**+.228**	-.041	+.044
Fund faith-based organizations	**+.461**	**+.304**	**+.239**	-.048	-.037
Allow prayer in schools	**+.590**	**+.404**	**+.307**	-.035	+.046
Liberal Agenda Items: Should the Government . . .					
Abolish the death penalty	**-.137**	+.010	**-.187**	-.015	-.007
Distribute wealth more evenly	**-.086**	**-.130**	**-.110**	-.037	-.032
Regulate business more closely	**-.103**	**-.056**	**-.079**	-.020	-.005
Protect the environment more	-.200	**-.174**	**-.139**	+.012	-.053
Promote affirmative action	-.003	-.008	**-.093**	+.014	-.089

Table 6: Baylor Religion Survey on correlations between religious indicators and political opinions (2006). Statistically significant numbers are in **bold type.**

Notice that those espousing biblical literalism have the largest correlations across the board—in favor of conservative and against liberal political agenda items. By contrast, Mainline Protestants are so diverse that none of the correlations is even significant. Much the same is true for Catholics. Evangelical Protestants are in between because they contain more biblical literalists.

The meeting of politically conservative religious people around biblical literalism is a point worthy of further reflection. Surveys have shown repeatedly that actively religious people are considerably more politically and morally conservative than others. What is less well known is that there is a three-way correlation between religiousness, conservatism, and authoritarianism. That is, the correlation between strong religiousness and conservatism is accompanied by a tolerance and appreciation for exercising authority and submitting to legitimate authority. Some solid research even suggests that this triple correlation of characteristics is partially heritable and cannot be completely explained by family environment. That is, by studying identical twins separated at birth and comparing them to genetically unrelated children raised in the same family, it is possible to conclude that there is a genetic as well as a social component to religiousness, conservatism, and authoritarianism (see the twin research of Laura Koenig at the University of Minnesota). Apparently, some people find the idea of the Bible as authoritative for their lives and for morality and social organization intrinsically, immediately appealing, and readily accept that it can be read literally as a timeless, decontextualized document.

This marks the right-edge border of the moderate middle territory we analyze in this book: biblical literalism crosses the line and is no longer moderate. Moderate Christians take the Bible not literally but seriously, as something with a claim on their lives and deserving prayerful study and careful interpretation. This defines a clear contrast with biblical literalists and also with the secularized liberal dismissal of the Bible's importance. It also implies a more complex view of the way that religious moderates should have an impact on politics.

POLITICAL AND ECONOMIC
INFLUENCES ON CHURCHES

We can ask the question of church-state relations from the other direction as well in terms of political and economic influences on religious groups. One of us recently visited a church and witnessed a meeting in which good-hearted Christians were trying to deal with a vague but persistent sense of dissatisfaction with their congregation. A few people in the room had specific complaints, but most were baffled by the whole situation. The newer folk in the congregation felt disturbed by the idea that the church they love might be beset by conflict of which they themselves had no inkling; they joined the church because it was everything they had been seeking. The people with a long history in the congregation seemed to be struggling with a changing church culture, and for some of them this was quite upsetting, even though they couldn't quite put their finger precisely on the problem.

As people young and old tried to articulate their sense of this change, one newer member spoke up. He gently suggested the political profile of the community and of the church membership was changing from its traditional liberal orientation to a mixed blend of liberals, moderate liberals, and moderate conservatives, and this transformation was transforming both the church's priorities and what people wanted from their senior minister. The comment was quickly passed over, perhaps because the subject was too touchy. If you are not supposed to talk about religion at a dinner party, then you are definitely not supposed to talk about politics in a church meeting.

We think this newer member's comment was on target. It compactly highlighted part of that church's ongoing experience of identity confusion. Once upon a time the fervently liberal members of this church might reasonably have expected wholehearted attacks from the pulpit on the social injustices of the American economic system, the evils of discrimination, the vulnerability of politics to corruption, the out-of-control military-industrial complex, and the horrors of war—all based in the powerful biblical heritage of prophetic social critique. Material acquisitiveness would have been diagnosed as greed and spiritual sickness—based on Jesus' own lifestyle and teaching. Social action on behalf of people suffering under political oppression, needless poverty, and avoidable disease would have been advocated in worship services and routinely supported in church budgeting and programs—based on biblical principles of dignity and justice.

Now things are different. There is no hostility to social justice efforts in the church, and the leadership supports existing programs and encourages new initiatives. But newer church members have brought different demands, and the minister finds them spiritually congenial; like attracts like. Thus, the sermons do not persuasively articulate the rationale for social-justice activity anymore, nor is the topic broached as often as in the past, because the minister's social justice instincts, while strong, are not as passionate as those of pastoral leaders from earlier decades. Rather, the social justice agenda has become diffused and exists alongside many other priorities where it has to fight off budget threats and personnel shortages. Because the minister does articulate the rationale for spiritual growth and prayer very persuasively, while the rationale for social action is comparatively less compelling, the unmistakable impression is that priorities have shifted. They have shifted, but not randomly.

The shift in priorities is a direct response to the spiritual and ideological sympathies between the minister and a newer generation of church members. Many of these newer folk are political moderates of a more conservative type than the church has typically seen. They want their minister, through worship services and sermons, to support their sense of respect for precious social and political institutions. They want the moral assurance that comes from biblical preaching. They long for the spiritual liveliness that a church proclaiming Jesus Christ as Savior and Lord can convey. They are not opposed to social justice any more than the minister is, and indeed they invest themselves in social justice projects. But they believe the church should be ideologically and theologically inclusive, and so the established social justice agenda has to share the stage with other concerns. The result is predictable: the older liberal members of the congregation feel disoriented by the lack of a compelling articulation of the rationale for social action. The newer moderate folk feel at home with the emphasis on spirituality and the relative lack of strident social critique from the pulpit.

This is a liberal church migrating toward the center—one way the liberal-evangelical church emerges from the political and religious left—and politics plays an important role in driving the transformation. This particular church will have to do a lot of work to define its emerging identity. It remains to be seen whether it can make the transition to an authentic liberal-evangelical congregation, one that strives to combine radical inclusiveness, prophetic social critique, passionate worship, and disciplined discipleship—one that places love and unity ahead of the comfort of socially potent like-mindedness.

The cultural divide in American Christianity sometimes involves religious crises much more dramatic than the subtle tensions illustrated in the previous story. For example, the Rev. Chan Chandler supposedly declared from the pulpit of East Waynesville Baptist Church in Waynesville, North Carolina, that anyone planning to vote for Senator John Kerry in the 2004 presidential election needed to repent or resign. Apparently this demand was based on Kerry's view that there should not be legal restriction of access to abortions, despite Kerry's personal moral disagreement with abortion. Rev. Chandler seems to have understood the contrasting policies of candidates Bush and Kerry on abortion to be the difference between good and evil—and surely it is the very essence of religion to stand for righteousness in the face of moral degeneration. Nine members of the 100-member church, including at least one Republican, allege they were removed from the church membership rolls because of their resistance to Rev. Chandler's demand that the church have a particular political identity. This triggered a painful conflict in the church, as the moderates asserted themselves against the minister. Forty other members resigned in protest. Rev. Chandler eventually resigned, remaining unapologetic and disputing his congregants' interpretation of the facts.

These situations are enormously painful, whether they are explicit collisions between politics and religion, as in the East Waynesville case, or subtle transformations in political sensibilities, as in the first example. But they fairly represent some of the ways that the liberal-conservative political and cultural divide can affect a congregation. Whether it is the wider national scene or a single church community, it is difficult to isolate theological and ecclesiological disagreements from their political and cultural contexts. Despite the wall of separation between church and state, religious groups frequently articulate political positions, especially on morally loaded issues such as military action and medical care, abortion and gay marriage; and the state routinely regulates the expression of religious convictions, whether it is prayer in schools or the display of the Ten Commandments in courthouses.

These overlaps between politics and religion magnify the liberal versus evangelical tension from a series of more or less in-house disagreements about doctrines and morals to a highly public battle with major political consequences. Moderates can feel lost in the middle, but their loyalty is to a stable and flexible social arrangement within which the third sector is in balance with the political and economic sectors. Moderates want religion to have a respected voice and a healthy moral influence without dominating politics and business. So they will push against religion on some issues and for religion on other issues. The appearance of inconsistency is misleading. Moderates need to learn how to articulate their guiding principles compactly and clearly so as to expose the deeper consistency of their intuitions about church-state relations.

CHAPTER 8

Morality and the Liberal-Conservative Conflict

We now return to the way the liberal-conservative tension in politics and religion reflects moral convictions as well as institutional roles and relationships. Gaining an understanding of differences in moral reasoning strategies between liberals and conservatives can go a long way toward easing the fighting and, at the same time, creating empathy among political enemies.

Textures of Moral Reasoning

Social psychologist Jonathan Haidt argues that we human beings construct rational moral arguments to make sense of intuitive, almost primal moral intuitions that are already deeply persuasive to us. He interprets his cross-cultural experiments and those of other experimental psychologists to indicate that moral reasoning arrives late to the party, after the emotions and moral intuitions are already in full swing. It is possible to develop conditioned responses that help us regulate the effects of deep-seated intuitive moral reactions. But Haidt says that typically only a tiny subset of highly educated intellectuals—the most objective among people professionally trained to be objective—ever really get proficient at making moral judgments based on moral reasoning rather than moral intuitions. That's how unnatural it is. For most of us, moral intuition is the heart and soul of our moral lives. Our moral judgments are intuitive responses to emotional moral reactions, such as respect or disgust, later backed up with reasons that explain why our intuitive judgments are sound.

Haidt identifies five cross-culturally universal domains of moral intuition that naturally stimulate appreciation for moral virtues. A few may be shared at some level with higher primates.

- The harm domain is associated with feelings of compassion, virtues such as kindness, and vices such as cruelty and neglect.
- The fairness domain is associated with feelings of gratitude and anger, virtues such as trustworthiness, and vices such as cheating.
- The in-group domain is associated with feelings of pride and belonging, virtues such as loyalty and patriotism, and vices such as betrayal.
- The authority domain is associated with feelings of respect and fear, virtues such as obedience and deference, and vices such as rebellion and disrespect.
- The purity domain is associated with feelings of satisfaction and disgust, virtues such as cleanliness and chastity, and vices such as tasteless and unnatural behavior.

A fascinating issue concerns the way these five domains of moral intuition became culturally universal, even while being expressed very differently in different cultures. There is considerable uncertainty about this. Haidt follows the conjecture of evolutionary psychology that basic domains of moral intuition were formed in the far evolutionary past, at a time when having moral intuitions in these five domains directly increased the probability of successful reproduction. We find debates over the origins of these domains of moral intuition interesting. But we are most interested in mining the experimental evidence for its contemporary relevance. In particular, we want to use this analysis of intuitive moral judgments to make sense of contemporary political polarization in the United States.

Haidt's research suggests that self-identifying liberals have been socialized to regulate morally loaded feelings that spring from the in-group, authority, and purity domains. Liberals learn to associate feelings of disgust with cruel treatment of people who seem different, and so they endeavor to be tolerant. Similarly, liberals link in-group feelings with racism and xenophobia and authoritarian feelings with sexism and abuse, so they stay on their guard against them. Liberals still have feelings from these three domains but try to prevent them from determining their moral judgments. Instead, they emphasize the domains of harm and fairness. In emphasizing the virtues of doing no harm and being fair to others, liberals intuitively support a simpler and less textured moral system. Haidt calls it a "thin" morality.

By contrast, self-identified conservatives treat all five domains with roughly equal importance, making for a "thick" morality. This means, for example, that conservatives tend to trust that their feelings of disgust indicate the morally wrong, whereas liberals would be suspicious of the moral value of such feelings. Similarly, loyalty to one's group and deference to figures of authority are virtues prized in conservative moral frameworks because these virtues help to sustain the valuable institutional social arrangements that help us to flourish.

Thin and Thick Moralities in Action

As an example of the contrast between liberal and conservative styles of moral reasoning, consider the following reconstruction of a conversation one of our colleagues had with a friend.

Lenny is a by-the-book liberal with a moral framework that heavily subordinates in-group, authority, and purity moral intuitions to those from the harm and fairness domains. He values empathy and fairness above all and is suspicious of virtues such as loyalty to the group and deference to authority because he believes they have often led to enormous abuses of those who seem different. He is not a bumper-sticker sort of guy, but he smiles with understanding when he sees "Resist Authority" plastered

on the back of other cars. Charles is a conservative whose moral
intuitions and reasoning have a thick texture in just the way that
Haidt describes. He treasures social stability as the condition of
personal fulfillment and deeply believes that loyalty, deference,
and purity are essential for preserving the wonders of civilization. Charles feels quite annoyed when he sees those "Resist Authority" bumper stickers. Both are well educated, affluent, and
active in the same local church.

Lenny and Charles are friends and particularly enjoy watching football together. One day they get to talking about the butt-
slapping that goes on after a play, and before you know it they are
discussing homosexuality. This is a new topic for their friendship
so they cautiously carry on a stop-and-start conversation when
there is no action in the game. They quickly discover that they
disagree about gay marriage. Charles supports a constitutional
amendment to protect traditional one man–one woman marriage,
while Lenny thinks justice and compassion demand letting gays
marry. They are not surprised by this disagreement because they
are used to disagreeing about politics. But then Charles, after
checking to make sure the kids are not around, leans in toward
Lenny and says in a low voice, "I feel totally disgusted at the
thought of anal intercourse, especially between two men. In fact,
I feel that way about any sex act between men. It seems totally
unnatural to me; it goes against the grain of nature." Lenny says,
"Me, too." Charles's brow immediately furrows. "What do you
mean?" he asks. "How can you feel the same way as me about
gay sex and still carry on about gay rights and gay marriage?"
Lenny pauses. He knows this is serious because they are talking
quietly while a football play is under way.

Lenny eventually turned to his earnest friend and said, "I
guess I don't trust my feeling of disgust the way you do. I think
feelings like that often lead to discrimination against people who
are different through no fault of their own. And so I try to set
my disgust aside and concentrate on empathizing with gays and
making sure I don't treat them unfairly." Charles digests this for
a minute. They watch another play in silence. Then he says, "OK.
It's weird to split yourself in parts like that, trusting some bits
but not others. I think God gave me a conscience, and I should

trust it, period. But I get where you're coming from about moral intuitions going haywire and leading to injustice. That's why slavery never felt wrong to too many Americans for such a long time."

As in this conversation, the conservative will often assume the feeling of disgust rightly indicates the moral badness of the acts in question. The liberal will usually assume people have different sexual tastes, and the disgust reaction has to be subordinated to virtues of compassion and fairness so as to avoid discriminating against people who simply are different. This is a complicated matter and can't be settled by making fun of the opposition. Rather, realizing we have different textures of moral intuition and reasoning, and knowing these sorts of moral and political contrasts have persisted throughout the history of human civilization, we are better able to understand the political and moral Other.

WHY ARE THERE DIFFERENCES IN MORAL REASONING?

Why are liberals willing to subordinate the in-group, authority, and purity domains of moral intuition to the harm and fairness domains? There are several levels of answers.

- On the level of social conditioning, they have learned from experience to see the harm and injustice caused by intuitive moral judgments springing from what Haidt calls the in-group, authority, and purity domains. So they train themselves and their children to regulate moral intuitions in those domains even though they may still experience the associated feelings, just as Lenny described.
- On the level of social context, liberals tend to live in cosmopolitan environments with high diversity and mobility, which puts them in touch with diverse people with obviously different customs and tastes. The only way to manage such a social arrangement is by de-emphasizing the in-group, authority, and purity domains of moral intuition because they interfere with smooth social

functioning in pluralistic, highly mobile environments. You don't expect sophisticated in-group customs of deference and greeting from a foreign merchant, and because you want to do business you don't demand it.

- On the level of psychological temperament, other research shows that liberals tend to like variety and appreciate openness. They are the teenagers who can't wait to leave the country town for the big city or to attend college on one of the cosmopolitan coasts.

Why do conservatives tend to preserve all five domains of moral intuition and fight for a culture and lifestyle in which all five domains make sense? Allowing all five domains to play a role in intuitive moral reasoning is more or less the default mode for human beings. When conservatives observe the lifestyles of cosmopolitan, mobile people through firsthand experience or through the media, they tend to feel a barrage of negative emotions that signal the violations of precious virtues that truly work in their own social contexts. Of course, it is often the extremes of cosmopolitan life that attract the overpoweringly negative reactions, but that is enough to confirm the conservative intuition that protecting the richly textured moral fabric of familiar social life is crucially important.

We particularly appreciate the way Haidt's analysis inspires sympathy and understanding across the lines of battle. His theory is statistical in nature, of course, so it follows that there will be individual exceptions. But it offers a sound, empirically based explanation for one of the deepest agonies of cultural disagreements over morality. Rather than continually feeling lost in the middle on moral issues, moderates can learn from Haidt's analysis that they are committed to dynamic balancing of moral intuitions against other considerations relevant to moral reasoning. They tend to believe that moral intuitions in some cases lead us to the good and true and beautiful, but, in other cases, badly mislead us. Moderates accept this as part of the human condition and systematically refuse to oversimplify moral reasoning in the way that both ends of the political-moral spectrum tend to do.

Everyone can benefit from interpretative frameworks such as Haidt's because they can recognize both themselves and others in the schema. This aids mutual understanding and perhaps might even inspire constructive compromise on key moral questions. It is particularly valuable for the liberal-evangelical church. Stressful encounters with the Other, striving for understanding, and enduring moral transformation are experiences at the very core of liberal-evangelical churches. Haidt's model helps us both to picture the sorts of challenges such churches can expect to confront and to conceive ways to work through them by acknowledging differences under the command to love one another.

Haidt's framework also helps us to articulate the senses in which Christian churches sometimes conform to cultural norms for moral behavior when they should be striving for the countercultural moral lifestyle intimated in the life and teaching of Jesus. The senses in which Jesus' command to "love your enemies" is countercultural are so much clearer in light of this analysis of the intuitive moral reactions of human beings, especially in the authority and in-group domains. In short, *Jesus' morality does not readily fit our normal ways of moral thinking and feeling*. That is what makes it difficult and radical and important.

A Moderate Conclusion

If you are a moderate Christian of the liberal-evangelical type, how might the information about politics in the chapters of Part III affect your self-understanding? What can you do, practically and positively, about this new self-understanding?

First, regarding self-understanding, if you are a moderate Christian, you are probably a political moderate also. You may be a Republican, Democrat, or Independent, but you are among the moderates in each of those diverse camps. You are used to discerning genuine value in the opinions of those with whom you disagree, and you sometimes feel annoyed by political true believers who seem unable to do that. You probably feel that the liberal-conservative split in politics, as it is currently amplified in our so-called culture war, has gone too far. You long not for ideologically ideal liberal or conservative political leadership but for honest and wise political leaders with a talent for statecraft and an ability to rouse in people a sense for the difficult but wise middle course in politics, economics, social organization, and international relations.

Moderate Christians of the liberal-evangelical kind are used to being caught in the political cross fire. They see how easy it is to succumb to polarization in politics because one-sided rhetoric is everywhere, and they do not always know just how to explain their complex political viewpoints in a compact and compelling way. But that is where knowledge and self-awareness can really help. Our reflections on the three deepest reasons for the liberal versus conservative conflict in politics—different institutional expectations, different views of church-society relations, and different textures of moral reasoning—have the potential to transform the self-understanding of moderate Christians. Seeing the fundamental political fight in this way inspires empathy, which feels just right to most moderate Christians. After all, one of the reasons they are moderate—and remain moderate—is that they easily glimpse wisdom in opposing camps and so are glad to see a theoretical framework that helps to explain political polarization.

Second, regarding action, *the practical and positive next step is to use what you have learned to help those around you increase empathy for their political opponents.* The move from frustrated confusion to knowledgeable empathy is empowering. Knowing what they stand for and how to express it to others can help moderate Christians become an articulate and compelling voice for understanding and empathy within society.

In the last two decades, it appears the influence of Christian churches on wider cultural life has declined markedly. George Barna's research rates the seven dominant forms of influence on culture as movies, music, television, books, internet, law, and family life. Less dominant but still important influences on the fabric of cultural life are schools, peer groups, newspapers, radio, and the business world. Local churches lag far behind all of these influences. The church has squandered its moral influence on internal squabbling and moral hypocrisy, and many people are now paying only limited attention to what church leaders, church organizations, church publications, and faithful church members say. It takes a self-aware communicator with a clear message to get through this haze of disillusionment and have any impact on the political or economic sectors of contemporary life.

In short, *as a moderate Christian you can become an articulate spokesperson for moderation and depth in politics and religion.* Through conversations with others, you can increase the mutual understanding and respect that you long to see in your society. You can be transformed from feeling lost in the middle to being a force for political transformation, economic responsibility, and religious tolerance through mutual understanding.

PART IV

We're Different, and That's OK . . . Except When It's Not

CHAPTER 9

Basic Sociological Principles

To the existential, demographic, and political perspectives of earlier parts, Part IV now adds a sociological perspective on the liberal versus evangelical conflict and the meaning of being lost in the middle between the two sides.

Sociology aims at providing objective descriptions of human group dynamics. Its objectivity has been challenged by theologians in books such as John Milbank's *Theology and Social Theory: Beyond Secular Reason*. But we think sociology can be relatively objective in one sense: it describes religious groups and discerns basic patterns in their dynamics—information on which both supporters and detractors of religion can agree. The question of religious truth is distinguishable from these considerations.

Sociologists have learned a great deal about the way human groups work. Sociologists studying religion have discovered that what they know applies to religious groups as well as to any other groups. So we do well to pay attention to the basic human dynamics that condition group life. Accordingly, we confine ourselves here mostly to basic sociological descriptions and principles that have won wide agreement from people with very different assessments of the value of religion. Yet we want to insist that human creativity and determination also makes it possible for human beings, empowered by their religious beliefs, to run against the sociological probabilities and to forge groups whose social identity does not comfortably conform to the standard models. This is the sort of community the Christian church often aspires to be: a beacon on a hill that shows the power of love to unite people despite their differences.

In our time, when some churches use sociological wisdom to develop church growth techniques, and others fall victim to hard sociological realities as they wither and die, we think the liberal-evangelical church is the right place to be. It is there that love within the community becomes stronger than theological differences, and worship binds more tightly than political ideology. Sociology is a doorway not only into the dynamics of religious groups but also into diagnosing the countercultural character of a moderate Christian church committed to unity and radical inclusiveness in its message and practices.

THE NEED TO BELONG AND RELIGION

People need to belong. This is the most basic fact of social life. It is not true of snakes and spiders and other species that spend the majority of their days alone. But it is true of ants and penguins and whales, of elephants and dogs and chimpanzees. And it is true of human beings. We are a social species, and when we find a place to belong, we need to feel at home there. That means minimizing feelings of discomfort by trying to get along with others. It means finding ways to enforce the commitment of individuals to group goals. It means detecting freeloaders and punishing insincere fakers who try to take advantage of group benefits without offering anything significant in return. It means minimizing confusing experiences of cognitive dissonance that disturb peace of mind and threaten corporate solidarity. We can tolerate a few fights and a few disagreements, but if there are too many of them and we start feeling intensely uncomfortable, then it may be easier to withdraw or, if there are alternatives, to find another place to belong and learn to feel at home there instead. These are the very building blocks of sociology.

Whatever else they may be, churches are social groups to which people belong and in which they strive to feel at home. In fact, in churches this need to belong has cosmic dimensions and ultimate significance. For in church the question of belonging has fundamentally to do with being at home with God and feeling morally and spiritually oriented in the complicated world we inhabit. That world is made a home for Christians precisely because the church teaches them how to perceive it as the creation of the One in whom we live and move and have our very being (Acts 17:28), the One with whom human beings are ultimately most at home. This visceral experience of vertical, cosmic belonging facilitates the potent horizontal, social aspects of belonging and vice versa.

Sociologists have long studied the role of religion in helping people belong. For example, Peter Berger's *Sacred Canopy: A Sociological Theory of Religion* explains how the human need to belong leads us to organize the world into the sort of place in which we can feel at home. For each society, this involves the construction of a social reality, including core values and habitual practices that are so obvious to us that we scarcely notice them. Even when we do see them we typically will not realize that they are constructed. When we try to participate in another culture, however, we suddenly stop feeling at home because we no longer know how to live effortlessly, comfortably, automatically. We feel like fish out of water and quickly come to realize how much we depend on our familiar environment in order to feel at home in the world.

When Berger analyzes the transparency of our social world, he notices several phases in an ongoing cycle of social construction and maintenance. We externalize our socially constructed world through cultural and political expression. We objectify it in groups and languages, in institutions and laws. Then we internalize this social world, from the time we are babies, absorbing its norms and rituals and becoming expert at speaking and acting within it. The worlds we create are complex, so it takes a couple of decades to figure out precisely how to move through them with grace and style. That is what we mean by the maturing process, and most of us get there eventually.

We might not like the way our world bites back, as when we get stuck in traffic jams, can't pay our bills, or have to defer to those above us in social hierarchies regardless of the quality of their ideas. But with a bit of effort, we can also see how much our social worlds enable us to do relatively conveniently. We can meet most strangers without fear. We can organize bustling economies. We can communicate efficiently. We can meet and marry and procreate without too much trauma. None of these blessings—including even the last—is true of many other social species. The social organization of reality is the key to belonging, coping, and feeling at home in the world.

Every now and again, something goes seriously haywire, and the fluency of our social participation stops. We are physically attacked by a stranger or by someone we thought we could trust. War breaks out and there is chaos where once there was order and security. We become seriously ill and suddenly face our own finitude. Our child dies from an accident due to taking needless risks. Perhaps the social structures we take pride in turn evil. At such moments, we realize that coping and feeling at home are not just about externalizing, objectifying, and internalizing a social world. There is a chaotic aspect of reality we dare not face without the protection of belonging. Berger calls it *anomia*—the lawless part of reality that scares us. Like cave dwellers huddled around a fire for protection from known and unknown dangers of the night, our social worlds serve to tame the world, or at least to make our encounters with the untamed parts of it relatively rare.

We invest formidable amounts of energy in attempting to tame *anomia*. But even in societies where health care is good, accidents are rare, and violence is kept in check, we still encounter the uncertain chaos of reality. Those encounters are often life-changing moments. If you haven't had moments like this in your own life, just ask a rape survivor, a battle-tested soldier coping with post-traumatic stress, or parents who buried their child.

Religion helps us cope with the parts of reality that are out of our control. In Berger's phrase, our world is not only a social construction; it is also a sacred canopy. Sacred canopies include religious narratives that explain why chaotic events occur. They teach us how to relate ourselves rightly to powerful beings such as gods and angels and demons that can protect us and care for us or else harm us. Like a vast film projector that uses the infinite sky as its screen, sacred canopies boldly write the order of our social world into the wider cosmic order of reality. They explain how the laws of our local culture are not arbitrary but truly the laws of the universe itself, and thus we are obliged to obey them and must not challenge them. They present our religious and life rituals not merely as our own creations but as mandated by God, and thus we are obliged to perform them.

Elevating our socially constructed worlds into sacred canopies is the human way of taming the uncertain chaos of reality. Even the most ardent antireligious person, when face-to-face with the horrors of uncontrollable *anomia*, longs for a way to think about it that makes reality a home rather than a hostile wasteland with lucky islands of life. Karl Marx seems to have been correct that the pain and suffering of this world provokes religious beliefs in a supernatural other world, which then helps us to cope. In that sense religion may well be a symptom of the social and economic sicknesses that cause our suffering, just as he claimed.

This much virtually all sociologists can accept. Moving beyond description, however, religious beliefs add a vital evaluative element—different for different people and traditions, obviously. Here is what we believe. Behind all social malfunctions and all economic injustice, beneath the fragility of biological life, the chaos of uncontrollable events, and the certainty of suffering and death, we find *God encountered and engaged through it all*. Religion is not only a symptom of suffering, as Marx thought. It is also an *authentic response* to suffering. We can accept the sociological description of religion's role in the social construction of reality and still affirm the *value and truth of religious belief*. This is not a sociological statement but a theological one. It makes a big difference in the way religious people appropriate sociological theories. Religion as the cosmic projection of a socially constructed reality can sound cynical and hostile toward religion until we realize that this accurately describes the way human beings operate *and* that we can engage ultimate reality authentically by operating in this way.

SURVIVAL INSTINCTS AND CULTURAL ASPIRATIONS

The basic social drives we have been describing are powered by survival instincts that spontaneously produce in human beings self-protective behaviors. Survival instincts indirectly inspire the nurture and defense of kin, who share our genetic heritage. Protective feelings make us wary and ready either to run for safety or to stand and fight when the situation demands it. They make us cluster in groups for protection and allow into the group only those people we feel we can or must trust with our lives. They make us vigilant about the resources of food and water we need to survive and willing to fight if necessary to protect those resources.

We often think of self-protection, vigilance, suspicion, and hostility as morally questionable behaviors. Yet they are evident everywhere in social life, and it is only civilized social realities that mask their presence. The veneer of civilization sometimes fails, and such failures are well documented in books and movies if we haven't lived through them ourselves. At such moments, the presence of self-protection, vigilance, suspicion, and hostility is completely obvious. The very point of civilization, from one perspective, is to give people what they need so that they don't need to fight for it and so that they can keep negative feelings and dangerous behaviors firmly in check.

Layered on top of these basic social drives and survival instincts are more refined cultural aspirations. We want to create music and art, organize societies, establish justice, right wrongs, have adventures, make discoveries, fall in love, unearth the meaning of our lives, and become fully actualized people. These drives push us toward cooperation and tolerance of differences, because we have to work together to achieve the loftiest of our cultural goals.

Our cultural aspirations often line up with our survival instincts. For example, it is easier to indulge in the culturally ornate survival ritual of buying food at a modern supermarket, so long as you have money, than it is to hunt and kill and cook animals or to sow and tend and reap grains and vegetables. Yet the desire to cooperate is also in dynamic tension with the drive to survive. Cooperation requires tolerance of differences, while survival demands suspicion of differences. Cooperation requires uncomfortably subordinating our own interests to the group's overall goals, while survival promotes greater comfort within a small, like-minded group. Cooperation requires sharing resources widely and relying on broad economic arrangements to ensure justice and fair distribution, but survival allows each small group to guarantee that its immediate survival needs are met.

THE REALITY OF SIN AND RELIGIOUS RESPONSES

Somewhere in the tension between cultural aspirations and survival instincts, the realities of selfishness and insecurity, violence and cruelty, and sloth and stupidity afflict human life. It is not surprising that sin should rear its ugly head, given the delicate balance of pressures that has to be maintained for social harmony and peace. But the effects of sin are terrible. Social systems, no matter how useful, are unjust. Economies, no matter how well planned, do not distribute resources fairly. Political leaders are sometimes corrupt and through nationalist fervor or social coercion can drive their people into wars of murderous aggression and revenge and theft. Violent conflicts over resources and religion and over cultural differences and freedom are disastrous and common.

Sensing this magnificent and tragic tapestry of human life, most people long to make things better rather than worse. (It is important to remember that some religious people thrive on conflict and pray for the collapse of civilization and the end of the world. But this, too, is a passionate response to the tragic tapestry of human life, ultimately seeking to make things better through supernatural intervention.) We long to experience the harmony and unity we can imagine but never quite see around us. In our families we long to be close to one another, but we also fight for the love and support we need, and we fall into depression or become furious when others frustrate our longings. In the wider society, we long for justice and peace, for social conditions that give children a chance to thrive on love rather than merely survive neglect, for kindness and patience in place of harshness and anger, for peaceful relations between nations based on common understanding and shared interests. We can imagine it, we can almost taste it, but somehow it perpetually eludes us.

Religions promote various ways to handle this human condition. They try to model alternative visions in communities and look to religious heroes as examples. Christianity points to the life of Jesus and to Christian martyrs and saints for inspiration. It tries to nurture the message of God's love and justice within the life of the church. Sometimes it has even tried running societies although with mixed results. Many people turn to Christ and the Christian church because they find there a haven for their sorrows, healing for their own failure in the tasks of life, and a place to nurture their longings for a just and peaceful world. Just as they want their own lives to manifest love and peace, so they want their church to model unity and tolerance so that it can be a source of genuine hope for the world.

Religions, then, have potent roles in several phases of human social dynamics.

- Religion is a key resource for giving cosmic dimension and comprehensiveness to our social constructions of reality.
- Religion's legitimating power makes it a source for the authority that some covet for the sake of social control and to which many others long to submit for the sake of making the world comprehensible and manageable.
- Religion numbs us to suffering, helping us forget and fail to see, but it also helps us notice and respond to suffering in healthy ways.
- Religion is the power source for personal transformation toward visions of goodness that transcend the ordinary selfishness of natural social life.
- Religion supports human corporate life by nurturing moral visions in the lives of adherents.

CHAPTER 10

Core Message Pluralism

Sociological principles help to explain why church unity can be very difficult to achieve, as well as why it is socially important. To understand the practical social and spiritual difficulties confronting moderate Christians and churches, however, we need to add another dimension. This is the problem of core message pluralism. To explain core message pluralism and its effects on social cohesion and group identity, we need to discuss what holds groups together.

The Bonding Power of Love

We have said people need to feel at home where they belong. Love makes people feel at home more than anything else. This is a tough message in a culture that tells us we can feel at home if we buy enough stuff and if we change ourselves and our bodies to fit in with those we admire or envy. Perhaps the greatest lie is that, if we can only perfect our technology, we can shield ourselves more perfectly than ever before from the natural processes of death and disease, aging and suffering. In the clamor of such delusions, in the harsh blare of brazenly cynical commoditization and "thingification" of human lives, our need for love is a still, small voice. It is the voice we badly need to hear, and it speaks the only word that finally matters to us. It quietly, relentlessly contradicts what the advertisers and magazine publishers tell us, denies what the politicians promise us, and deconstructs the message of accumulation and consumerism the economic system furiously insists we embrace. The still, small voice simply reminds us of what we knew in our parents' arms as children, if we were fortunate to find love there. It tells us divine love reaches toward us from every direction, graciously accepting us as we are, and gently inviting us to love others as we have been loved.

The prophetic power of the message of love's ultimate centrality in our lives is truly stunning. It unmasks our pretentious and bizarre ways of denying our simple need to love and to be loved. But we know full well how difficult it is to live into, and to live up to, this vision of love. In practice, love does not heal all wounds and unite us across all differences. It might, but it does not. And we cannot help but suspect the problem lies with us rather than with the ideal of unconquerable benevolence that is divine love, especially as conceived through the biblical portrayals of Jesus. Our emotional needs make selflessness difficult to achieve, even when we actually experience the satisfaction of selfless acts of kindness. Our social instincts make unity in difference hard to maintain in the long run despite the fact that we often look back on moments of such togetherness as among the most memorable of our entire lives.

Christian life is not just about biblical and spiritual ideals. It is also about coming to terms with the practical realities of human finitude and sin. Most Christians believe we can never be perfect, so we need to know how to become better while still coping with failure. We know the Christian church cannot be completely united globally or locally, so we need to know how to find our way toward humble transcending of differences in love even while living with the disappointment of fractious fights and denominational divisions. Love may be the ideal answer to what makes human beings feel at home in the world, therefore, but it is not the only answer in practice.

THE UNIFYING POWER OF SHARED BELIEFS

As much as anything, and especially in churches, solid core beliefs held in common promote strong group cohesion. In the short term, it does not matter much whether those beliefs are right or wrong. An unwavering commitment to a particular belief system holds people together—it holds groups together—and it can also hold an individual together through the challenges of life. This is especially because the legitimating force of cosmic religious narratives depends on everyone in the group accepting the stories. Groups have to minimize questions about plausibility that induce uncomfortable cognitive dissonance.

At the individual level, when core beliefs are challenged, we can feel intensely threatened. Without a trusty belief system to guide us, life quickly becomes uncertain, unexplainable, and radically uncomfortable. We can take the world and its unexpected twists and turns in stride and strive for a graceful movement through uncertainty. But this is exceptionally difficult to achieve. Something similar happens at the group level. Consensus around core beliefs is a vital element of a cohesive group identity and that includes church groups. A group can handle a period of uncertainty about its narratives and central commitments, but it usually needs to sort out the confusion before too long if it is to hold together.

To drive home the importance of confidence in shared beliefs, consider the story of Nikki's encounter with a professor, Buzz, at a small liberal arts college in Pennsylvania. This encounter was a collision of worlds for Nikki and as unexpected as being rear-ended at a red light. Buzz was a wildly brilliant professor of biblical studies who believed that part of his educational mission was to break down the immature faith commitments of his naive students. This was a mission he took seriously and carried out with great care. Buzz loved his students and was easily the most popular teacher on campus, even though many of his students felt as though they were passing through the valley of the shadow of death when taking his courses. Nikki was a smart, attractive, born-again Christian in her first year of study. Wanting to learn more about her faith, Nikki made a point of filling her class schedule with Christian history and biblical studies classes. That's how Buzz and Nikki met.

Nikki sat quietly in her Introduction to New Testament class as Buzz showed all in attendance the contradictions in the birth

narratives of Jesus and the divergent accounts of Jesus' ministry
in the gospels. He argued that the New Testament was not a dis-
passionate journalistic account of events composed by objective
observers but the formational and foundational witness of early
Christians who believed intensely and often at great personal
cost. Most of the evangelicals in the class passionately objected
to Buzz's assertions, but his exhaustive knowledge of the biblical
texts always won the day. Buzz had no hesitation in presenting
evidence to crush fundamentalist arguments for the perfect authority and historical reliability of the Bible. But it was also obvious that he had great respect and enthusiasm for the Bible.

Nikki managed the gospels OK, but when Buzz turned his
attention to the Book of Revelation she began to feel uncomfortable. Buzz quickly and easily brushed aside the common
claim that the book had been written about the end of time in
our contemporary world, contending instead that John's Apoca-
lypse was written in response to the persecutions of early Christians by the Roman Empire using a special symbolic language
for self-protection from prying Roman eyes. Suddenly, Nikki's
belief that she was part of Jesus Christ's special end time revival
began to rattle on its foundation. She had grown up believing
she was "chosen" and therefore in service to God until Jesus
Christ was revealed in all his glory at the end of time, which
surely was near. Having read Hal Lindsey's books *The Late Great
Planet Earth* and *The Rapture,* and most of the Left Behind series
of novels, the idea that the Revelation of John was referring to
Rome and not to the evil empires of her own era was jarring. Yet,
as always, Buzz's arguments were convincing.

The section on Revelation was tough, but it was the discussion
of Paul's letter to the Romans that truly began to unravel Nikki.
Buzz spoke about Paul's concept of God's free gift of grace and
salvation. One of the students protested: to have eternal life—to
be saved—you need to confess with your lips and believe in your
heart that Jesus is Lord! Buzz began to make his case. "It's either
free, or it isn't. Free is free. Free means it costs nothing. There
is no cover charge—no secret password. If you have to make
a certain proclamation, then, while salvation may still be a
gift . . . it is simply not free." Then came the zinger for anyone

who attempted to interpret the Bible literally: "Your argument isn't with me. It is with Paul. It is with the Bible. I'm just telling you what it says. You can read it for yourself." That is when Nikki began to cry. The class stopped. Nikki hadn't uttered a sound all semester, and now the tears flowed. This smart, attractive, confident, young Christian woman had been reduced to a sobbing wreck. Under her breath she kept saying, "I don't know what to believe anymore. . . . I don't know what to believe."

Like so many professors, Buzz was better at breaking down a young person's faith than at helping to build it back up again. Buzz did not do this carelessly, which is what made his critiques so devastating. Nikki knew Buzz cared about her development as a person of faith. He wanted to ensure his students left his class freed from the naïveté of their childhood faith while offering them the freedom to define their own faith journey in the future. But he did not offer much guidance himself.

Nikki's faith travels soon took her away from the church. If she couldn't believe in the Bible, then she couldn't believe in the church; and if she couldn't believe in the church, then what did that say about her belief in God? She tabled that question for years. She prayed most days, even while doubting that her prayers were heard at all. Years later, Nikki entered seminary and began to deal with her doubts about God. She found there not only convinced Christian believers but also seekers like her, struggling for self-understanding. Today she believes in Jesus Christ as her personal Lord and Savior, she believes in God as the creator of the universe, she accepts the Bible as authoritative for her life, and she believes in the power of prayer. Yet she also believes there is much about God and faith we can never know, that there are lots of valid ways of believing and acting as a Christian, that God's spirit works in every religion and every culture, and that the church must testify to divine love through radical inclusiveness and honesty about internal diversity of belief and practice. She knows what she believes, and those beliefs leave a lot of room for what she does *not* know.

Nikki fought her way to a vibrant faith by refusing the easy answers on her left and right and going deep instead. But on the way she felt the full terror of being rootless in belief and completely disoriented by a glimpse of the deep disagreements within the Christian faith about the Bible and theology. She knows with crystal clarity how important consensus on beliefs is for her own security and happiness. She understands how profound disagreements, and real knowledge of the actual diversity of Christian belief and practice, can tear a person and a church apart. But she also knows that faith has room for differences because of love, and the church has room for disagreement because of humility in the face of the infinite divine mystery. She still feels a longing for a grand Christian consensus of belief, but she understands the improbability of that ever occurring. For Nikki, the challenge of our era is to live faithfully and lovingly amid pluralism, resisting easy sloganeering, and testifying to the power of Christ's love to create love and community even where there is profound disagreement.

MISMATCHED GOSPELS

The unifying power of shared beliefs is undeniable. But what we have instead is pluralism of Christian belief and practice. We think that the deepest problem in trying to help moderate liberals and moderate evangelicals worship together and love one another is the simple fact that their gospels do not match. This is what we mean by *core message pluralism*. We sketched elements of the disagreement between the worldviews of liberals and evangelicals in Chapter 2, focusing on conflicting visions of reality, authority, history, morality, and church. How does that translate into their characteristic gospel narratives?

Evangelical theology defines a narrative context and a worldview for the core idea of being born again. The main elements of the narrative are:

- the severity of the problem of sin for human beings,
- our inability to do anything through thought or deed to save ourselves from this problem,
- a substitutionary theory of the atonement whereby Jesus dies for us and our sins in order to reconcile us with God,

- a conversion experience of repentance and being born again,
- a personal relationship with the living Jesus Christ,
- a personal idea of God as a being to whom we can relate now as well as for all eternity in the heavenly life to succeed this one, and
- the Bible as the authoritative source for this narrative and for all other matters of faith and morals.

Moderate evangelicals do not adjust this evangelical narrative framework very much, though they do reject a biblically literalist approach to understanding the authority of scripture.

For their part, liberals have stressed unity and learning, social work and compassion, freedom of opinion and spiritual diversity. They liberalized elements in the evangelical gospel and acknowledged pluralism in theology and church practice. They focused above all on the encompassing love of God and allowed variation on many other aspects of the Christian story.

Moderate liberals developed three practical principles to secure social unity in their pluralized form of Christianity. They did not usually give these principles names, as we do here, but their practices embodied the principles just the same.

- The *Principle of Humility* states that we human beings simply don't and can't know enough about divine matters to settle all questions, not even in the light of divine revelation.
- The *Principle of Love* states that Christians should cleave to one another unconditionally, accepting and loving each person for who he or she is.
- The *Principle of Christ-Centeredness* states that Christianity is about Jesus Christ, not picky debates over details of belief and practice; it is more about devoted discipleship than doctrinal details.

These principles make room in the church for plural understandings of the gospel even while protecting Christian unity. There is also room for the fabulous diversity of spiritual practices evident

within the history of Christianity. Moderate liberal Christians believe that openhearted humility, unconditional love, and Christ-
centeredness will keep the church together in spite of the disruption caused by acknowledging core message pluralism.

It is true: these gospels really do not match. We might think
we could turn to the Bible to sort out this disagreement among
moderate evangelicals and moderate liberals about the Christian
gospel. But it was precisely close study of the Bible that produced
core message pluralism in the first place. It does not take a seasoned biblical scholar to notice the New Testament has colorfully
different formulations of Christianity's core message, and none
of them is much like the official creedal Christianity of the fourth
and fifth centuries, despite continuities that persist through the
development of doctrine. The most obvious and famous contrast
is between Jesus' preaching of the Kingdom of God and Paul's
preaching of Christ crucified; the evangelical gospel sounds a lot
more like Paul than Jesus. Neither of those is much like Peter's
preaching to Jews as recorded in Acts 2, in which the crucifix-
ion and resurrection are not primarily about salvation but about
injustice and God's reversal of it, confirming Jesus' authority,
his message, and his identity as the Christ. Hebrews presents a
technology of sacrifice that bears little resemblance to James's
vision of Christian salvation. We also have the much later doctrinal articulations of the Trinity (three persons in one substance)
and hypostatic union (Jesus Christ is truly divine and truly human). These doctrinal formulations articulate the good news using Greek metaphysics in a way that is quite alien to the simple
stories of the Bible. The changes in Christian practice during the
same period are as important as those in theology.

Once they discover it, even though it may bother them, *most
moderate Christians want to take core message pluralism seriously*, basically because they love and respect the Bible and don't want to
delude themselves. But how can they do this without losing their
evangelical identity, with its dependence on consensus around a
plain gospel story? Can we free up ("liberalize") some parts of
the evangelical gospel to reflect the core message pluralism of
Bible and Christian tradition? Can we recognize the different rec-

onciliation theories within the New Testament and subsequent Christian thought? Can we accept similar variation in ideas of divinity? Is it viable to go in the opposite direction from conservative evangelicals on the authority of the Bible, seeing it as a sacred but culturally conditioned source of revelation and rejecting inerrancy and literalism? Can the church hold strong without basic agreement on such points?

These questions are about sociological possibilities and probabilities, as well as about theological truth. The sociological answer is clear up to a point: acknowledging core message pluralism definitely makes forging a coherent social identity more difficult. Any church taking on this challenge will face an uphill battle to hold together. Many people choose churches that confirm their prejudices rather than challenge their beliefs. This decision supports greater core message unity and comfort and confidence. Acknowledging core message pluralism moves in the *opposite* direction, and that is just asking for trouble. An important question for moderate Christians, therefore, is *how much diversity is too much?*

THE NEED FOR A COMPELLING MESSAGE

In the last half century, the social success of evangelical Christian denominations has been as obvious as the decline of mainline and liberal denominations. There are exceptions. Diana Butler Bass has done a wonderful job of describing some of them in her book, *Christianity for the Rest of Us*, which is a study of inclusive mainline congregations that are flourishing—and many of them are of the liberal-evangelical variety. But the broad trends still matter for assessing sociological dynamics and likelihoods. Numerous studies point out that social cohesion and shared beliefs are keys to social success.

Evangelical Christianity has a better glue for social life. This glue may not make the kind of flexible bond liberals are used to, but it holds diverse people close together and fosters the heat that starts the fire that changes lives. The recipe for the glue is simple enough, and there is good evidence that the principles involved are common to human beings whatever their social and religious framework. Here it is.

There must be a compelling message. The core message must make a convincing story, one that captures imaginations with its grandeur and richness, its historic boldness and prophetic edge. It must make sense to children and yet unfold onto endlessly fascinating details. It must be memorable. It must be practical and immediately relevant to the existential struggles of our lives. It must conjure new perceptions—what Swiss theologian Karl Barth called the "strange, new world of the Bible"—that change the way we look at the world we think we know. It must be told often in creatively diverse but consistently reinforcing ways. Core beliefs and practices must be keyed directly into the narrative elements of the message. Corporate life must involve energetic worship linked closely to the message and must focus attention on personal growth in faith, bonding experiences of sharing faith with other believers, adrenaline-rush experiences of sharing faith with those outside the group, and explicit demands of the group on the individual.

This recipe works, and not just in Christian churches. As we have seen, however, there is a big problem: core message pluralism *complicates the message* and thus *weakens the social glue* that is the secret to evangelical Christianity's attractiveness. Intuitively sensing this social disaster right on the heels of every challenge to the coherence of Christianity's core message, evangelical groups typically let challengers know—quickly and in no uncertain terms—what "the group" believes. They often tolerate curiosity and diversity. But when group identity is in danger, it is common to see strategies of control such as appeals to authority, subtle accusations of disloyalty, the implicit or explicit threat of social marginalization, and actually casting out those who don't fit. If liberals typically migrate to evangelical settings full of stiff awkwardness but eager for some real excitement and amazed at the energy they find, evangelicals often arrive in liberal land feeling seriously beat up and stunned that there is a place where they are loved for who they are and their personal views are welcomed.

Pluralism at the heart of the Christian movement is an immovable problem. Do we celebrate the pluralism but lose social cohesion in the process? Or deny the pluralism in order to preserve the tie that binds? This kind of catch-22 is not that uncommon in life. But life and institutions alike are about dynamic balance and adjustment, not static perfection. This is the deepest theological reason why liberalism and evangelicalism need each other: like yin and yang, they are complementary.

How does a moderate church of the liberal-evangelical sort brew the glue and hold the center even while admitting there is more than one way of reading the Bible, more than one formulation of the core message of Christianity, and more than one way to live as a faithful Christian? We have heard answers to this question that amount to "Let's celebrate our diversity!" We have to do that, certainly, but this is blessedly naive as a strategy for maintaining social cohesion.

There has to be another way. It has to be a compelling way that avoids the intellectual sins of liberal fudging and evangelical oversimplification. It must be a socially realistic way that creates excitement and changes lives without committing the social sins of suppressing diversity and boring people witless. It needs to be a spiritually vital way that rejects the dual sins of avoiding spiritual depth through compassionate social outreach and neglecting the world in the name of individualistic salvation. Above all, there must be a powerful message that can become the story of liberal-evangelical churches and the life story of discerning moderate Christians.

We think liberal-evangelical Christians do have a powerful narrative for guiding life and inspiring Christian unity. We will go right to the heart of this core narrative by showing what it means to place radical inclusiveness ahead of doctrinal purity.

RIGHTLY ORDERED PRINCIPLES

For the reasons we have been discussing, church leaders are often caught up in the principles of faith, grappling with rules that define and exclude. They have good reasons to do this. Churches need principles to define their identity, to know what to do and how to treasure their heritage. That is good and necessary, theologically and spiritually as well as socially. Christians need to know that they follow Jesus Christ, that their self-understanding springs from the Bible, and that they live under the double command to love God with all their heart and mind and soul and strength and their neighbors as themselves. But some principles actually get in the way of authentic Christian life, first becoming fragile in their unreasonableness and then shattering on the unyielding facts of everyday experience.

That is why the average moderate Christian layperson approaches faith at a more practical level, where principles and rules are woven into the fabric of life, with all kinds of accommodations and exceptions. "The church says I can't have an abortion and I can't use birth control. How am I going to enjoy my sexual life with seventeen children to feed and put through college? I have to find another way." "The pastor says all Muslims are going to hell, but my Islamic neighbor prays five times a day and loves his wife, while my Christian neighbor swears at his kids and beats his wife. I think my pastor is a bit extreme." "Jesus is hardly ever mentioned in our worship services and our church is dying—we don't know how we are going to pay the electrical bill. The new church in the industrial park talks about Jesus all the time, and they have had to hire a patrolman to direct traffic at their entrance on Sunday mornings . . . maybe we should start talking about Jesus."

Most moderate Christians live in the in-between place where principle and practice constantly adjust to each another. But plenty of hard-nosed church leaders quickly diagnose this kind of mutual adjustment as a compromise of the Christian gospel, an accommodation to cultural norms that destroys the integrity of Christ's church. In place of flexibility over church-defining principles, they reassert the rules: "You can't have an abortion and you can't use birth control and that's that!" "All Muslims are going to hell and that's that!" "We don't do enthusiastic Jesus-talk at our church and that's that!" We have some sympathy for the policy of resisting cultural accommodation. But it is vitally

important to draw the right line in the sand, to order our principles of Christian identity in the correct way.

To illustrate concretely, we relay a story about a couple we
know. Jean and Dick are Roman Catholic. They attend Mass several times a week without fail. They feed the homeless a ham
and bean supper every Wednesday evening in the basement
of their church. They are proud great-grandparents who make
family a priority. Throughout their marriage of thirty-two years,
they have been as devoted a couple as one could imagine. Yet
Jean and Dick did not receive communion for more than half a
century. Dick's first marriage had been to a Protestant woman
who died in a car accident, and Jean's first marriage ended in
divorce. The Protestant marriage and the divorce dictated that
neither Dick nor Jean could receive communion at their church.
All those years ago the priest told them they were not allowed
communion, and the two obediently stayed away from the altar.
In fact, their new priest would likely have told them that they
were welcome at the table, but Jean and Dick were so deferen-
tial that they never thought to ask, and the priest did not know
their history and neglected to inquire about this strange situation. When the congregation would move forward to take Mass
each week, Dick and Jean would remain in their seats feeling
shunned and sinful.

Frustrated and heartbroken by this exclusion, there was a time
when Dick and Jean considered leaving their church altogether.
They had some friends who had been nagging them about at-
tending another church, and one Sunday they finally went. The
contemporary worship service was so completely different from
their church experience that it was unsettling for Dick and Jean,
but the worst part was when people learned they were Catholic.
Someone told the pastor, and the pastor invited Dick and Jean
into his study after the service in an attempt to "save" them.
Feeling even more judged than they had at their Catholic church,
they decided to visit a Mainline Protestant church in the center of
town. People there were friendly but not outgoing. The bulletin
cover proclaimed "You are Welcome Here," and in the sermon
the pastor preached about how we were all created equal and

how we should treat all people justly. But, something was missing: the church didn't even offer communion. Dick and Jean left feeling as empty as ever.

That spring Dick and Jean went to visit their grandchildren and great-grandchildren. On Sunday the entire family went to a liberal-evangelical church. The word of God was read and preached, and communion was celebrated as it was every week. The invitation to the Eucharist was both Christ centered and inclusive:

> This is the Lord's table. Therefore, the invitation cannot come from a pastor, or a deacon, from our church council, or from any denomination. The invitation is from Jesus Christ himself and it is always the same—come as you are. Come as you are. It does not matter where you have been or where you are going, is does not matter what you have done in your life or what you have left undone, it doesn't matter whether you believe yourself a success or a failure, there is room for you at this table. The only thing you ever need in order to approach this table is a willingness to come forward. This is the Lord's table, and you are invited to make it your table.

Dick and Jean's grandchildren, knowing their history, fully expected their grandparents to remain in their seats. But Dick turned to Jean and said, "How can we not accept an invitation like that? I'm going forward."

On that spring day, Dick and Jean received communion for the first time in over fifty years. During the fellowship time after church, Dick and Jean's grandchildren introduced them to their pastor. The pastor heard Dick and Jean's story and encouraged them to return to their home church and talk to their new priest. The pastor suggested much had changed in the Catholic Church in the past fifty years, and he fully expected that Dick and Jean would be allowed once again to receive the Eucharist. To this day, Dick and Jean are devout Catholics. In fact, Dick is now a eucharistic minister for his parish, serving communion to members of their community who are homebound or hospitalized.

This terrible, wonderful story illustrates how rigidity over the wrong principles can be enormously harmful, while the application of rightly ordered principles can transform lives. Liberal-evangelical churches build their narrative identities around principles of radical inclusiveness and Christ-centeredness. They work hard to organize their core principles to accommodate practical realities, including core message pluralism and diverse Christian experiences, while remaining faithful to the gospel. These churches believe in Jesus Christ, and they take the Bible as a serious authority in their lives. Yet they recognize the complexity of God's creation and the expansiveness of God's grace. In Dick and Jean's case, the principle and practice of radical inclusiveness, inspired by Jesus' own ministry, had an immediately transforming effect in their lives.

CHAPTER 11

The Curious Social Strategy of Liberal-Evangelical Christianity

Christian churches and groups exhibit diverse social strategies. Most are triggered or influenced not only by historical circumstances but also by the double problem of core message pluralism and cultural diversity. Most have implications for whether and how Christianity should politically and morally engage the wider society. Relative to this array of options, the liberal-evangelical social strategy is unusual, and we will explain how this is so.

SOCIAL STRATEGIES OF THE MAJOR BRANCHES OF CHRISTIANITY

The major Christian divisions are so large that they sustain significant internal diversity and typically pursue a number of not necessarily consistent social strategies simultaneously. Because of its hierarchical global organization and ancient history, the Roman Catholic Church has the most consistently executed and clearly stated social policy among the large branches of Christianity. Authority is gathered up through priests and bishops and centralized in the pope. The bishops' and the pope's pronouncements on matters of doctrine and morals define the core identity of the Catholic Church, and the hierarchy has decisive authority to maintain this core identity through resolving all disputes and weeding out intellectuals, priests, and lay leaders whose words and actions threaten it.

If Catholics don't like this policy—and many do object to the teachings on women and married priests—they have the option to leave. This was not a feasible option in most medieval villages, but it is possible in the modern world. If Catholics leave, however, won't the church shrink? Pope Benedict XVI made it abundantly clear shortly after taking office that a smaller and purer Church is not necessarily a bad thing. In the Catholic social strategy, the core identity of the church must be protected at all costs. Around that core the Church sustains an impressive array of diverse activities with room for many kinds of people. As long as Catholics sign on to the core identity and do not challenge church authority, they can do almost anything they want to do in the various activities of the Church. Part of that core identity is coming together in the sacrament of the Mass to worship in a way that makes sense no matter where in the world they may travel.

It is difficult for other Christian groups to duplicate the social strategy of the Catholic Church, no matter how large they are and how much they envy its identity-defining power and prophetic focus. They simply do not have the global reach, the hierarchical organization, the lengthy multicultural heritage, and the sheer numbers needed to define identity in the way the Catholic Church does. Interestingly, the Mormon Church perhaps comes closest with its global reach and clear hierarchy.

The Eastern Orthodox Church is a communion of more than a dozen national or regional self-ruling hierarchical churches. The Orthodox celebrate their organization as a communion of self-ruling churches because it gives substance to their central theological affirmation that Christ is the sole head of the church. Yet this organizational form has also made it difficult for the Eastern Orthodox Church to muster unanimous moral force. They are virtually unanimous on questions of doctrine, but the histories of the various Orthodox churches have produced sharp political disagreements that cannot easily be resolved, and there is no pope to impose an authoritative solution where people cannot agree.

This, on an international scale, is like the problem facing churches locally when they have a liberal-evangelical commitment to unity among moderate Christians across ideological and theological differences. Any communion of moderate Christians seeking to transcend political polarization in the name of testifying to the transformative power of divine love will be burdened with a social liability, namely that ordinary human power politics cannot be the main resource for achieving unity. Without the indirect and sometimes direct coercion of hierarchical power, it is difficult to define a clear identity and achieve a definite moral stance.

Mainline Protestant denominations are struggling for a clear identity. Organizations such as the World Council of Churches and the World Alliance of Reformed Churches have very little impact on defining Christian identity for Protestant denominations, Protestant congregations, and Protestant Christians. It is said that few members of Rick Warren's Saddleback megachurch in Southern California know about its Southern Baptist connections, and most of the few who do don't care. The same is true of many church members even when the sign outside the church makes the denominational connections obvious. Mainline denominations recognize the problem and routinely hold conferences to strategize about defining and strengthening their identity. But only the minority who are passionate about their denominational heritage attend those conferences, and it is difficult to leverage much change in the consciousness of the denominationally indifferent majority.

This social reality thoroughly dilutes the prophetic moral message of Mainline Protestants, much to the frustration of denominational leaders, who struggle in vain to help their denominations forge meaningful identities. The unrelenting disagreement among Protestant Christians on everything from theology and morality to politics and economics makes consensus on anything virtually impossible to achieve. As a result, Mainline Protestant denominations have sacrificed their moral influence and usually meekly reflect positions already present in the wider political fights of the day.

Hidden in this disaster of mainline Protestant denominations is the great social strength of local, congregation-based Christianity—a core asset in all forms of Christianity but especially in Protestantism. The efforts of denominational leaders to define corporate identity notwithstanding, Protestant Christianity is predominantly about engaging the world congregation by congregation, community by community, family by family, Christian by Christian. Mainline congregations typically know their local congregational history better than they know the history of their denomination. Protestant Christians move more easily than ever among congregations, most feeling little sense of betrayal if they cross denominational boundaries. Along the way, Christians live out their faith and exercise an enormous influence on their communities, their workplaces, and their families. As in the era when Christianity was born, most important spiritual events occur in congregations of Christians who worship and serve God together.

The trend is clear: there is little stable middle ground for ecclesial social strategy between the proven extremes of Roman Catholic hierarchy and local congregational energy. Denominational leaders will rightly continue their fight for stable middle-level organizational structures, but their efforts will probably enjoy only limited success.

BEYOND THE MAJOR BRANCHES

The brave new world of the denominational church in a pluralistic environment involves building transitory supra-congregational structures with defined purposes that assemble themselves when needed and can dissolve without any real harm to the church when their time has passed. Such organizational strategies are amply evident in the shifting alliances of evangelical congregations outside the mainline denominations. They are now expanding as mainline denominations seek to survive their precipitous membership declines and aging populations.

Some Protestant Christians give up on denominations and join groups so unconstrained by other Christian bodies that their options for creative social strategies increase a hundredfold. Some of these are tiny and have little impact on the wider society but sustain themselves in neighborhoods as storefront churches and community churches. Others, such as Pat Robertson's Christian Broadcasting Network and the 700 Club, have massive impact because they leverage the media to influence Christians whose primary identity is in a local congregation. Still others, including intellectuals such as Stanley Hauerwas and religious ideologues such as Rousas Rushdoony, have idiosyncratic visions that persuade a few loyal followers (we discuss these figures below). The result is a rainforest-like tangle of astonishing social life-forms.

Some social strategies stress separation and self-containment. For example, Amish communities nurture prized values in economically and socially self-sustaining communities. Their religious hope lies not in the transformation of the wider world but in the purification of their souls before a holy God. Anabaptist theological ethicist Stanley Hauerwas understands the church to be a separated people whose moral obligations and otherworldly vision utterly transcend any human economic and social arrangement. Thus, he takes Christian pacifism seriously and sees in the Christian gospel a perpetual critique of human power and self-reliance.

More moderate than Hauerwas is theologian George Lindbeck, who defends a view that can be called "postliberal communitarianism." This view insists the world of Christians is difficult to translate into wider social terms. It has its own language game whose grammar is doctrines, and it supports its native life patterns in the form of distinctive liturgical practices. The church has to find its distinctive identity within its own heritage of beliefs and practices, not in dialogue with cultural fashions.

Similar to Lindbeck is radical orthodoxy. Like the Anglican Oxford Movement in the nineteenth century, radical orthodoxy is a contemporary Anglican movement that presses for a deeper engagement with what its proponents deem to be the native resources of the Christian tradition. This is based on supreme confidence that Christian teachings are uniquely powerful and true, that they speak with a single voice with no substantive conflicts, and that they can never be reduced to other forms of human wisdom. Radical orthodoxy asserts that Christianity has a unique social vision and so Christians should do things the Christian way without apologizing for being different or strange relative to ways of life in the wider culture.

Other social strategies are almost opposite to those and have bold political aspirations. The most well known among these is the social strategy of ultra-fundamentalists (Robert J. Marzano's term) such as the late Jerry Falwell of the Moral Majority, James Dobson's Focus on the Family, Tony Perkins's Family Research Council, and Pat Robertson's Christian Coalition. With relatively minor differences, each in this group seeks to establish a theocracy, which is a form of social organization in which God alone is the ruler. This necessarily involves eliminating alternatives, and that makes many opponents nervous. Even more extreme is the reconstructionist dominionism of the late Rousas Rushdoony and others. Dominionists believe that the Old Testament provides a legal framework for Christian societies, and they attempt peacefully to change laws to match those of the Old Testament. This is the Christian equivalent of Islamic sharia law.

Some social strategies are essentially otherworldly in orientation. They regard this world as under the dominion of Satan and impossible to restore or improve. Unlike the Dominionists' postmillennialism, in which Christ only returns after a glorious thousand-year reign within human societies, these otherworldly views are premillennialist. They believe the world will degenerate steadily into depravity and evil until Christ intervenes to destroy evil by force and establish his thousand-year reign in a new heaven and a new Earth. The classic example of this in our time is the fundamentalist premillennialism of Tim LaHaye, most famously articulated in the Left Behind series of novels, as well as movies, comics, and other spin-offs. These are highly influential books; the 2006 Baylor Religion Survey reports that a staggering 19 percent of Americans—that's almost sixty million people—have read at least one of the books in the Left Behind series. Though there is some question about the influence of these terrifying yet engrossing novels on people's religious views, this size readership probably means that premillennialism is as popular now as it ever has been in the United States.

Finally, there is a variety of cultural engagement strategies that emphasize prophetic speech and transformative action in society based on a religious vision of how it should be. Among Catholics, classic examples are Dorothy Day's nonviolent activism and Pope John Paul II's use of Catholic political muscle. Among Protestants, a classic example is the liberal accommodationism espoused by Ernst Troeltsch and others that aims to make the gospel comprehensible in each new context. Accommodation to cultural norms and practices always occurs within the church, even when the church in question trumpets an absolute policy of nonaccommodation. The social novelty of liberal accommodationism was to name this constant adjustment for what it is and to make a virtue of striving for self-conscious decision making about how the church should change over time.

Most recently, Jim Wallis and others have held forth on behalf of progressive evangelicalism, which perpetuates the social activism traditions within evangelicalism—an agenda that is closer to liberal than conservative in today's political terms. Rather than withdrawing from the world, Wallis and his Sojourner's community urge evangelical Christians to engage and transform it. This neatly coincides with liberal evangelicalism at the moral level, though Wallis leaves theological questions mostly implicit in his best-selling *God's Politics*. That book has a readership of almost four million people within the United States as of the early part of 2006, according to the Baylor Religion Survey. This size readership strongly suggests that the book hit the mark and helped progressive Christians express their frustration with American politics. Here we see another social strategy at work: changing the imaginations of individual Christians and churches in the name of a particular social vision.

BEYOND THE CHURCHES

Moving outside the Christian world we see other social strategies for relating religion to society and for managing religious and cultural pluralism. We will pause to comment on just two instructive examples.

First, the accidents of modern history have caused the contemporary divisions of Judaism to line up more closely along liberal-conservative lines. The nineteenth-century Reform movement insisted that Jewish people should engage the world, move out of the ghettos using the new freedoms guaranteed by secular states, claim their national identity wherever they lived, and transcend superstitious interpretations of the Torah. The conservatives objected and aimed for a more moderate reform of medieval European Judaism that sustained a clearly recognizable Jewish identity. The so-called orthodox never bought into this debate at all but continued the old ways.

The contrast with Christianity is notable, as most of the mainline denominations include both liberal and conservative elements together. Whereas this arrangement produces enormous tensions within Christian denominations, the functional divisions with Judaism more or less resolve these natural tensions automatically. Should Christianity reorganize itself and divide into new denominations that separate liberals from conservatives? In fact, this seems to be what is happening, given the shrinking and aging of mainline denominations. But this is safer when the religion is a minority religion. A culturally dominant religion divided so as to match the geography of culture wars could potentially destabilize a nation.

The final social strategy for managing religious and cultural pluralism that we will mention is an utterly secular one, with its own kind of logic and appeal. We think it is neatly expressed in the lyrics of Terri Clark's country song, "I Think the World Needs a Drink" (© 2005 John D. Lewis and Dawn M. Lewis): "I think the world needs a drink / I think enough's enough / She's been spinnin' around so long, I'd say she's pretty wound up / Calm down, sit back, relax / Tear up the contracts an' save the ink / Yeah, I think the world needs a drink." We do not mean this as a joke. The real wisdom here is that people can often work out their differences through conversation in which they do not take themselves so seriously. This marks a sharp contrast with, and a critique of, the way religions tend to magnify and intensify disagreements to the point that conversation seems utterly pointless. This, in turn, is why secular people think of religion as the single biggest reason that human beings cannot solve their problems and why secular humanists yearn for an era where religious passion takes second place to social responsibility and respectful conversation. Think of John Lennon's famous song "Imagine" in which he dreams of a world without countries, hunger, and war, and no religion, too.

Christians need not agree with the social policy expressed here—indeed, one of us is of Methodist heritage and does not drink alcohol!—but all of us should ponder the critique of religious passion that it indirectly conveys. Maybe we can get farther by stressing patient listening and a sense of humor than by demanding that heaven rain down fire and brimstone upon our enemies. For moderates who stress Christ-centered radical inclusiveness, religion is less about the passions of certainty and more about the patience of empathy.

THE LIBERAL-EVANGELICAL SOCIAL STRATEGY

This greatly abbreviated cook's tour of social strategies helps us appreciate the social strategy of liberal-evangelical churches. Liberal-evangelical Christianity self-consciously embraces a significant degree of pluralism and the predictable difficulties that come with it. This is for the sake of establishing what liberal-evangelicals believe is a desperately needed witness to love's power to unite a plural church and diverse cultures. Instead of lining up with sociologically common forms of religious organization, liberal-evangelical Christians and congregations deliberately include moderate liberal and moderate evangelical Christians in their midst, even though the congregation that results may threaten to burst apart at the seams under pressure from wider cultural and political battles. Through worshiping together they seek to testify to the unifying love of Christ, which is what keeps them together.

Sociologist Christian Smith presents one way to estimate the probabilities against which liberal-evangelical churches must strive in his *American Evangelicalism: Embattled and Thriving.* Smith's analytical framework for explaining evangelical vitality is a version of competitive marketing theory. The standard version focuses on the way elites exercise the power of organizations to nurture and protect their interests in relation to competitors. Smith enhances competitive marketing theory to handle the beliefs and actions of ordinary Christian believers as they struggle to relate to a pluralistic cultural environment—he calls this the "new paradigm." Seen in this framework, the secret of evangelicalism's success is its passionate engagement of a pluralistic culture; pluralism inspires evangelicalism to thrive through forcing it to compete with many other beliefs about the world, about values, and about faith.

Smith's subcultural identity theory of religious persistence and strength is persuasive, and his book has been warmly received as a result. It explains why being embattled helps evangelicalism to thrive. This in turn shows why including liberals who want to be radically inclusive will cause problems: their inclusive beliefs will decrease the intensity of evangelicalism's embattled subcultural identity. Smith mentions the problems some Christians have with exclusive evangelical beliefs and their frustration with ongoing evangelical failure to live up to Jesus' ideal of radical inclusiveness and agape love. Unfortunately, his model does not take sufficient account of these perspectives. In fact, these contrary reactions are the power sources for liberal-evangelical faith and church life. Despite this problem, Smith's model does show that *the liberal-evangelical church must run against the sociological odds*. And that makes the social strategy of liberal-evangelical Christianity a curious one.

There are some limits on the degree of diversity the liberal-evangelical church can sustain. In relation to the right, liberal-evangelical churches do not allow their appreciation for biblical authority to be voiced in terms of biblical literalism. Biblical literalists are welcome in the community, but the view is criticized publicly. In relation to the left, liberal-evangelical churches do not allow Christ to lose centrality or the Bible to be marginalized in theory or practice. Christians for whom Jesus Christ is an optional aspect of faith are welcome in the community, but Christ and Christian discipleship are front and center in worship and preaching. Similarly, Christians who do not take the Bible as a serious authority for faith and life are welcome in the community, but they will see the authority of the Bible demonstrated through the biblical emphases of educational programs and preaching.

These limits do not rule out any moderate Christians, at least as we define them. But they do recognize that there are practical limits on the ideals of Christian unity and Christian love across ideological and theological lines. Liberal-evangelical congregations go against the sociological odds, but they do not attempt the sociologically impossible.

Positively, moderate Christians of the liberal-evangelical type believe divine love conjures reconciliation in many places and ways. In the Middle East it is through programs that enable Jewish and Palestinian children to spend time together and learn about each other. In Northern Ireland it is through social movements that enable Protestants and Catholics to work together. In the context of North American culture wars, it is through moderate Christians who worship together even if their moral instincts and political views are opposed on hot-button issues.

The liberal-evangelical social strategy probably can never be the basis for a trans-congregational denominational identity. But at the level of single congregations it can and does work very well. In particular, it satisfies the yearning of moderate Christians to worship and serve God in a way that places Christian identity ahead of political identity and love ahead of comfort.

A Moderate Conclusion

If you are a moderate Christian of the liberal-evangelical type, how might the sociological information in the chapters of Part IV affect your self-understanding? What can you do, practically and positively, about this new self-understanding?

First, regarding self-understanding, we think there can be something liberating about recognizing the sociological dynamics of religious groups. When Christian infighting seems avoidable or optional, we can get locked into accusations and blaming. When we see the bigger picture, the fights take on an almost timeless and inevitable aspect. Seeing this allows us to be more generous to opponents on all sides. For example, understanding the deleterious effects of core message pluralism on the identity formation and maintenance of Christian groups helps moderates understand why conservative evangelicals and fundamentalists often deny that core message pluralism even exists and why liberals often surrender to a relativized pluralism of Christian opinions in which anything goes. With that understanding in place, it is easier to appreciate the resulting social strategies and even to empathize with those whose social strategies strike moderates as more or less disastrous.

From this position of empathy and understanding, moderate Christians of the liberal-evangelical kind can see clearly how dramatic their distinctive quest is for radically inclusive yet Christ-centered churches. This quest demands a kind of unity that swims upstream against a culture of low-conflict groups customized for comfort. It flies in the face of the sociologist's group-feasibility statistics. It strives to create a witness to the unifying power of divine love in a world that seems deeply skeptical, a world that usually prefers hostility and revenge to peacemaking and cultivating empathy across political and religious differences.

This defines the sense in which moderate Christians with liberal-evangelical aspirations are *truly radical* in their religious convictions. Their social goals are deeply countercultural and strike at the very heart of the human inability to love the Other. Moderates can take this radical social and spiritual agenda as one of their personal life goals and as a serious corporate objective. The sociological perspective of this chapter is a good starting point for assembling the basic conceptual tools needed to articulate those aims in a compelling way.

Second, regarding action, most people experience two practical challenges when they try to act on this liberal-evangelical approach to church unity. On the one hand, there is a challenge with relationships. In a liberal-evangelical church, moderates may find themselves worshiping and praying next to someone whose political views really bother them, whose supernatural worldview dismays them, whose naturalistic approach to religion outrages them, or whose sexual orientation disturbs them.

This is where the rubber meets the road for liberal-evangelical congregations. Can they commit to Christian fellowship and love despite such awkward disagreements? Do they experience humility and thankfulness for one another in prayer and at the communion table? That is just too big a challenge for some people. But for the liberal-evangelical Christian it is precisely the challenge they seek. Nothing less can testify to their convictions about the power of divine love to unite fractious human beings in love. *Rising to this challenge requires deliberately cultivating empathy for others through often repeated practices of prayerful self-awareness, open discussion, and working side by side with those who differ politically and theologically from us.*

On the other hand, there is an individual challenge. Acknowledging core-message pluralism in the way required to participate fully in a liberal-evangelical congregation can be spiritually confusing. For some people it weakens confidence in the foundations of Christian faith. The solution to this difficulty is the same one we recommended at the end of Part I's discussion of existential challenges: a lifelong commitment to radical discipleship, humble learning, and compassionate social engagement. There are no shortcuts to this kind of spiritual maturity.

One of us recalls teaching a Christian education class introducing the New Testament to two dozen eager adult learners. In the course of discussing the various writings and trying to get on the inside of each document to appreciate its perspective on Christ, church, and gospel, a significant split developed in the group. Two people were extremely disturbed by the class's attempt to honor each biblical author and to allow each book to have a profound impact on our lives. They sensed that the impact was different from book to book, which interfered with their conviction that there could be absolutely no pluralism in the core message of Christianity. These two went on the attack in order to defend their conviction that the Bible had a single divine author and so was free from the influence of human perspectives and social contexts. Meanwhile, the large majority of the class was transformed by the experience, thrilled to experience the New Testament's inspiring claim on their lives and determined to study it more closely in the future.

Acknowledging core message pluralism is not easy for some, and it can be spiritually disturbing for almost everyone at first. With time and practice, however, allowing the Bible's diverse voices to speak to us enriches the experience of reading it. As we gain a sense for the diversity of the Christian tradition, core message pluralism becomes less disturbing and gradually feels more like something for which we can be extremely grateful. This in turn gives us the basis for acknowledging the Bible's authority in our lives in a practical, commonsense way. Moderates accept the challenge not just to *cope* with core message pluralism but also to *appreciate* it and see it as one of the *great strengths* of their liberal-evangelical faith. Rising to this challenge requires actually reading and studying the Bible, learning about church history, and appreciating the diverse faith perspectives of others in our religious communities.

PART V

Reclaiming a Noble Heritage

CHAPTER 12

Early History

We have argued that the coexistence of moderate liberals and moderate evangelicals within a church community presents a much-needed opportunity to demonstrate unity against the grain of cultural divisions. It sets a lamp of love on a pedestal and lets it shine (Matthew 5:14-16). The simplicity of this testimony is truly compelling ("This little light of mine, I'm gonna let it shine") and has inspired every evangelical movement and every loving act of self-sacrifice throughout the history of Christianity. The Christian touchstone for the testimony of love is Jesus' own life and ministry, the numerous kind touches, looks, and words that transformed the suffering and sadness of those he met, and especially the Bible's moving description of his acceptance in love of a brutal execution (Luke 22:41-42). We desperately need such signs of love. Communities that make this witness resist the social reflex to split whenever pluralism makes them uncomfortable. This is the very effort that many Christians feel called to make.

The liberal-evangelical longing to unite apparently conflicting theological and political instincts has deep historical roots. In fact, we find utterly fascinating the origins and history of evangelicalism and liberalism, the pressures driving their separation, and noble past attempts to resist the resulting conflict. Sometimes words such as "liberal" and evangelical" can become semantic cages. Seeing how the meanings of these words have changed with time and circumstance can help us break out of our cages and picture new possibilities. Knowing the relevant history can inspire discerning moderate Christians to claim both sides of their identity with open hands and thankful hearts. Moderate Christians of our era are not the first to prize unity above ideological correctness and fanatical purity in the church. Others have gone before us, and we can learn from them.

THE ORIGINS OF EVANGELICALISM

Evangelicalism usually refers to a modern movement. We'll get to that, eventually, but we first reach back into the heritage of the word "evangel" itself. This will situate the evangelical movement in its proper historic place and explain why evangelicals chose that name.

Let's begin with some etymology. Any good dictionary will lay out the basic history. The word *evangelium* is a Latinized transliteration of the Greek compound noun, eu-angelion, which appears in various forms throughout the New Testament. The prefix means "good" and the main part of the word, which yields our word "angel," simply means messenger. The word refers to the good message as well as to the welcome messenger who brings it. "How beautiful upon the mountains are the feet of the messenger who announces peace, who brings good news" (Isaiah 52:7).

Evangel is a synonym of "gospel," which is a word with a strange history. More than a thousand years ago, Old English speakers needed to explain the Latin "evangelium" in plain terms, and they came up with the word "gospel." How did that happen? They translated the parts: "ev" came from the Greek "eu" and went to the Old English word "god," meaning good. The word "angelium" came from the Greek "angelion" and went to the Old English "spel," meaning announcement. If you think about the word "spel" you will see that this is not surprising. "Spel" came from the Greek verb "spillon," meaning to announce, and all of the senses of our word "spell" reflect that root meaning. When you put the pieces together, what do you get? God-spel. Yes, this explains the name of the famous 1971 rock musical *Godspell*, a whimsical portrayal of Jesus based on the Gospel of Matthew.

"Gospel" is a pronounceable version of god-spel and means good announcement, matching the Latin and Greek roots perfectly.

Why do we usually say "gospel" rather than "evangel"? "Gospel" caught on in Old English because of a pun. The Old English word *god*, meaning "good," is similar in pronunciation to the quite distinct Old English word *god*, meaning "God." The relationship is still evident in today's English, with the extra "o" in "good" carrying forward the different vowel sound from a millennium ago. So *gospel* began its life meaning "good announcement" but quickly came to suggest "God's good news." It was a happy coincidence. An evangelical is a "god-speller": one who announces God's story of good news in Jesus Christ.

The politically charged modern history of the word "evangelical" has grown atop this native cluster of meanings. It began when sixteenth-century Reformers used it to designate the beliefs they thought were proper to the true gospel, as opposed to both corrupt Catholic belief and deviant heretics among their Protestant brothers and sisters. Catholics used "Catholic" in the same way, of course. Used in this oppositional way, it was a bold act of linguistic theft, dramatically narrowing the scope of the gospel. "Evangelical" now referred not simply to the evangel, the Good News in Jesus Christ, but much more specifically to *our correct version* of it, specifically against *our enemies' distorted version* of the Good News. It was a "we" versus "they" situation, with one version of the gospel opposed to other versions in the name of doctrinal orthodoxy, liturgical propriety, cultural identity, or ecclesiastical authority. Yet Christians could also unite under the "evangelical" name, even across denominations, because it stood for what they had in common. Thus, post-Reformation church leaders used "evangelical" both to authorize the "true" gospel and to consolidate Christian unity among like-minded Christians. The word has enjoyed these identity-defining and orthodoxy-assuring powers ever since.

The life of "evangelical" as an institutional name derives from these special powers; there was usually an enemy group of Christians somewhere in the picture, and there was usually recognition of a common evangelical heritage that united denominationally diverse Christians. For example, "evangelical" was and in some places still is used as a name for the Lutheran wing in contrast to the Reformed wing of Protestantism. An exception to this is the use of "evangelical" in the name for the 1817 union of Lutheran and Reformed churches in Prussia, but in that case the contrast group was German Catholics. This union is a classic expression of the ecumenical recognition of a shared evangelical heritage across denominational lines. At about the same time, it was the name for one of the leading groups in the Church of Scotland, opposed to the "moderates." It was the chosen name for a variety of American denominations, all wanting to distinguish themselves from the heresies of competitor Christian churches and all reaching out to one another in solidarity. In the Anglican Communion, where "evangelical" is increasingly widely used, it is virtually synonymous with "low church" piety, liturgy, biblical study, and doctrinal orthodoxy—contrasting with "high church" smells and bells and less emphasis on bible study and church doctrine.

"Evangelical" was also the name used for the early Methodist revivals in eighteenth-century England. In this context, the enemies of Methodism used the word to disparage its allegedly fanatically emotional and puritanical supporters. For their own reasons Methodists, and especially John Wesley, were happy to use it, too; it linked them to a heritage that transcended Christian denominations. Modern evangelicalism is sometimes traced back to John Wesley, with good reason. Wesley, like other evangelicals, derived a strong moral framework from pietism's instinct that our lives are lived transparently before God, with whom we have a personal relationship; sin is an in-your-divine-face insult to God. This led in his case to a radically biblical vision of justice and social transformation, which has been a characteristic of most evangelical movements ever since.

The association of the word "evangelical" with pietism also produced in some circles overtones of the moralist lifestyle and spiritual discipline typical of pietism and revivals, a layer of meaning it retains to this day. Ironically, many evangelicals of the twentieth century were no fonder of spiritual enthusiasm than those who poked fun at Methodist "evangelicals"; this indicates that the hints of religious-emotional excess in some usages of "evangelical" eventually dropped away, leaving suggestions of puritanical moral attitudes and pious spiritual discipline, along with an intellectual approach to Christian beliefs and more measured forms of spiritual fervor.

Behind mutual criticism of emotional Methodists and puritanical reformed folk, and beyond the revolutionary social justice and personal transformation agendas of early evangelicals, there was a deep common thread: second birth. Evangelicals were born again into life with Christ, borrowing an image from John's Gospel to describe this fundamental experience (John 3:1-10), and it is this line of continuity that links otherwise spiritually and theologically diverse groups of evangelicals.

As we saw in Chapter 10, the basic narrative framework of evangelicalism calls for a series of theological propositions that constitute a plausible worldview for the "born again" idea of reconciliation. This evangelical gospel narrative tells the story of how God saves human beings from sin through the atoning sacrifice of Jesus Christ on the cross. The sacrifice has to be a substitutionary death because the alienation of sin can be overcome in no other way. Once we accept this wondrous, divinely provided escape from the penalty for our sins, we enter into a personal relationship with Jesus Christ and daily learn how to relate to God.

The word "evangelical" has enjoyed its greatest staying power among groups that combine the elements we have discussed into a unified package:

- the group-defining oppositional elements,
- the denomination-transcending ecumenical elements,
- the morality-defining activism and piety elements,
- the stress on spiritual rebirth (being "born again"), and
- the theological framework that supports the reconciliation narrative

THE ORIGINS OF LIBERALISM

Liberalism has similarly fascinating origins. As with evangelicalism, however, most Christians understand liberalism with reference only to historically recent events, neglecting the rich heritage of the word and the ideas that resonate within it right down to the present day. So once again we begin with some basic etymology and medieval history.

In Latin *liber* means "free" and *liberalis* is an adjective describing a free person, by contrast with one who is obliged to serve others. The earliest uses of the word in English date back to the fourteenth and fifteenth centuries, where liberal described the arts, sciences, skills, and trades a free person could pursue. Because of this, the word *liberal* has had class connotations from the beginning. Once loosed from its explicit ties to medieval social hierarchy, "liberal" retained the idea of intellectual refinement in culture and learning. The ideal of freedom remained present especially in the possibility of not being narrowly restricted to specific professional training and thus able to explore, learn, and think whatever one would like. This sense of the world persists in the phrase "liberal arts" when college students explore a wide variety of subject matter with the intention of opening themselves to undiscovered possibilities.

A dual sense of freedom within "liberal" continues throughout the history of the word's usage. There is freedom *from* restrictions of lifestyle and convention and freedom *to* form opinions and act as we see fit, ideally guided by upper-class ideals of courtesy and compassion. In nineteenth-century politics, liberals sought freedom *from* strict adherence to founding documents such as constitutions and freedom *to* adapt to new social conditions, amending sacred constitutions as needed. In this case, the natural contrast was with political conservatives (though in contemporary U.S. politics it is the conservatives who want constitutional amendments). Nineteenth-century liberal Christians sought freedom *from* rigid creedal orthodoxy and strict adherence to stifling patterns of life while prizing freedom *to* explore the religious dimensions of science and art and literature, adapting traditional beliefs to contemporary circumstances.

The locus of authority for liberals is within rather than without. A liberal is self-reliant and works hard at cultivating a gyroscopic sense of morality and social responsibility. In medieval times a liberal or free man could choose a career rather than submit to existing rigid structures of society (women rarely had this privilege). In modern times, a liberal (man or woman) accepted responsibility for interpreting the Bible and receiving church tradition rather than submitting completely to the external authority of the Bible or tradition. This is the liberal's way of submitting wholly to God rather than to any intermediate or lesser thing. We saw in Part III that liberals tend to be exquisitely sensitive to the unintended disasters of human social and political arrangements and suspicious of those who assert the correctness of such arrangements on the basis of authority or tradition. Much the same is true in Christianity, where liberals believe the church can err, and it is up to faithful and insightful individuals of every era to chart a safe course between the existing wisdom of tradition and the new knowledge that arises in every generation.

The irony of the theological contrast between liberal and conservative is that the liberals of one era often hold beliefs similar to the conservatives of the next—in an earlier chapter we saw something similar with political opinions. Consider the classic varieties of liberalism famous in late-nineteenth-century European and North American Christianity. Most liberal Protestants held to a traditional creedal faith that is scarcely distinguishable from today's North American moderate conservative evangelicals. Similarly, most beliefs of liberal Catholics at the beginning of the twentieth century (the controversial so-called Modernists) are today taken for granted in mainstream Catholicism. Liberals may move too quickly and conservatives too slowly, but they do tend to move in the same direction, a generation or two apart. Liberals point to this ironic pattern as evidence they are neither opposed to tradition nor wrong in their beliefs but rather merely ahead of their time. Eventually, they say, even conservatives will think the same way.

CHAPTER 13

Modern History

It is against the early history described in the previous chapter that the more recent history of evangelicalism and liberalism unfolds. At the center of this modern history is the great evangelical split.

THE GREAT EVANGELICAL SPLIT

The eighteenth and nineteenth centuries saw the rise of scholarly approaches to the Bible—historical criticism, textual criticism, and literary criticism. Close literary analysis of the Bible is in fact an ancient practice that produced interpretative strategies such as the allegorical method, which allowed readers to treat nonliterally certain passages of Scripture that were deeply troubling if read literally according to plain sense. There are also faint traces of early historical criticism and signs of debates over textual authenticity. But these practices exploded toward the end of the eighteenth century, driven by the late Renaissance fascination with literature and history. By the end of the nineteenth century, these interpretative strategies had caused a widespread crisis in Christian assumptions about the nature and authority of the Bible.

Meanwhile, in the same period, scientific knowledge of the natural world grew rapidly, establishing a new way of finding out about reality. This new way of knowing was independent of biblical authority and ecclesiastical hierarchies. As the cultural prestige of science grew, so the assumption spread that we no longer needed supernaturally authorized knowledge to make sense of our world; we could answer questions about much of reality through science. We could get better medicine, better astronomy, better physics, better biology, and better technology through science than in any other way, including through paying attention to what the Bible and church officials have to say on those subjects.

Some Christians felt that new scientific theories directly challenged Christian beliefs. For example, there was great suspicion among many Christians toward British naturalist Charles Darwin's 1859 biological theory of evolution, though some Christian intellectuals were delighted with this new theory of the origin of species. In general during this time, Christian believers felt more comfortable expressing their doubts about biblical reports of miracles, their beliefs that certain parts of the Bible were mythological or serving special political interests in the early church, and their suspicions about the undesirable arbitrariness of religious authorities. This in turn eroded the plausibility of supernatural views of reality and forced Christians either to reassert supernaturalism against the cultural current (the path of the "traditionalists") or to accommodate Christian beliefs to scientific assumptions about what the world is really like (the path of the "modernists").

Evangelicals were caught on these issues. They discovered strong disagreements within their own ranks over how to respond to the rise of biblical criticism and the scientific study of the natural world. Being on all sides of every issue, evangelicals could not tolerate the resulting pluralism of opinion. This led to a long period of brewing controversy between traditionalists and modernists. The evangelical infighting grew steadily through the latter part of the nineteenth century, causing tension in all Christian denominations. It culminated in the early twentieth century with a decisive institutional break. As we shall see, it was Fundamentalists who led the way in this split, deliberately driving a dagger into the heart of Christian unity, which they took to be false and corrupt, in the name of doctrinal purity.

This split marked a new era for evangelicalism. Prior to the great evangelical split, the word "evangelical" carried memories of the Lutheran pietism of Philip Jakob Spener, the fervent Methodism of John Wesley and Phoebe Palmer, and the Brethren movement of Alexander Mack and the Great Awakenings in the United States. It expressed the theological commitments of most Mainline Protestant denominations, the fervor of evangelists such as Dwight L. Moody, and the very different passion of Christian intellectuals who could take biblical criticism and modern science seriously without feeling that they were compromising their evangelical commitments. Now the meaning of the word "evangelical" dramatically contracted to the traditionalist position, giving birth to the narrow connotations the word retains to this day.

Meanwhile, modernist evangelicals meekly allowed traditionalist evangelicals to steal the precious word "evangelical." The modernists were then called "liberals" rather than the fairer and the historically more accurate "liberal evangelicals" or "modernist evangelicals."

MODERN EVANGELICALISM

The immediate religious ancestors of those who first called themselves Fundamentalists made a prescient diagnosis of the difficulties into which Christianity was falling. They saw challenges to biblical authority as starting evangelical Christianity down a slippery slope. Once we make ourselves judges of the Bible, they reasoned, the Bible quickly loses its power to judge us. We can try holding our place on the slippery slope, but we can only do so with great effort and for a short time. Eventually, we slide all the way down to where the Bible is nothing more than a library of religious wisdom, compiled by people for the sake of preserving testimony to their culturally conditioned religious and ethical beliefs. The only solution, they argued, was to affirm the complete authority of the Bible. It is God's book, not a human library. It conveys God's own words to a world that badly needs to hear the divine message of judgment and redemption. We must defer to its authority absolutely. Biblical criticism and the scientific view of the world are irrelevant or worse.

Throughout the nineteenth century, traditionalism nurtured this authoritarian view in the major Protestant denominations. It existed alongside modernist views that welcomed biblical criticism, scientific knowledge, and the challenge of perching on the slippery slope. But the authoritarian view self-consciously opposed itself to modernism's ideal of balancing biblical authority and secular knowledge. Evangelicals were fighting among themselves, and increasingly believed the stakes were the very future of authentic Christianity.

From the time of its first meeting in Ontario in 1883, the Niagara Bible Conference met almost every year until 1897 to discuss the modernist versus traditionalist crisis, the rise of biblical criticism, and authentically biblical Christian doctrine. In this process they distilled the Niagara Creed, whose fourteen propositions were grounded in what the conference took to be the biblical view of Christian truth:

- plenary (i.e., complete) inspiration of the Bible;
- Holy Trinity;
- the fall and total depravity of human beings;
- transmission of original sin;
- necessity for salvation of being born again;
- redemption through the blood of Christ in a substitutionary sacrifice;
- salvation by faith alone;
- assurance of salvation;
- Christ focus of the entire Bible;
- church unity vested in union with Christ through baptism and the Holy Spirit;
- activity of the Holy Spirit;
- need for purity of the flesh;
- resurrection of the dead and eternal punishment; and
- premillennial second coming of Christ as the world degenerates into chaos and the church into apostasy.

The Niagara Bible Conference secured the trans-denominational identity of the traditionalist movement, which soon became the political base for Christian Fundamentalism. As its viewpoint hardened toward the end of the century, the conference also shrank in size, ejecting moderates from its membership. But it crystallized the most conservative viewpoint among the traditionalists into publications that then became reference points for subsequent debate.

At the same time, evangelicalism in a more classic, balanced, and practical form was powering influential student movements such as the InterVarsity Fellowship founded in 1877, the Student Christian Movement founded in 1889, and the World Student Christian Federation founded in 1895. This classic kind of evangelicalism was also at the root of the Young Men's Christian Association, which was founded earlier in 1844. It was the inspiration for the long-running ecumenical and evangelical Keswick Convention, which began in 1875 in England and continues to this day. It was the 1946 Keswick Convention that decisively influenced Billy Graham's faith and message.

These evangelical movements formed the imaginations of a new generation of evangelical leaders. While traditionalist in doctrinal matters, they tended to be ecumenical in outlook. They stressed the social action and second birth aspects of modern evangelicalism and tended to avoid hard-edged formulations of doctrine because they rightly felt that they interfere with the proclamation of the gospel. It is in the contrast between these groups and hard-edged groups such as the Niagara Bible Conference at the end of the nineteenth century that we see the first signs of what would become a new round of fighting among traditionalists. But at the time of the great evangelical split, their interests aligned to some degree because of the need to resist modernism.

Influenced by the Niagara Bible Conference, but working specifically from the Westminster Confession of Faith, the 1910 General Assembly of the Presbyterian Church distilled a slightly different list of five fundamental beliefs that were to give Fundamentalism its name. Probably intended as much to counter some of the extremes in the Niagara Creed (such as its explicit premillennialism) as to affirm traditionalism, the Presbyterian list of "five fundamentals" was:

- inerrancy of the Bible;
- virgin birth and deity of Christ;
- substitutionary atonement;
- bodily resurrection of Jesus, and
- authenticity of Jesus' miracles

These five fundamentals were the centerpiece of twelve volumes of ninety-four essays by Christian scholars entitled *The Fundamentals: A Testimony to the Truth*, edited by R. A. Torrey and others, and published between 1910 and 1915. Many of the sixty-four contributors were influenced by the Niagara Bible Conference and its creed, and they explicitly rejected the main tenets of biblical criticism, which modernist evangelicals accepted. The *Fundamentals* aimed to provide denominational and church leaders with the intellectual and conceptual resources needed to combat the errors of modernism in their own churches. This target audience underlines the trans-denominational character of early Fundamentalism. The project was funded by some wealthy oil barons, who gave enough money to publish and send three million copies of the entire set of *The Fundamentals* to Christian leaders in the United States.

With the rise of Fundamentalism came two developments for evangelicals. First, Fundamentalists crystallized the contrast between traditionalism and modernism that was causing intense internal conflict among evangelicals generally. With names for the conflicting positions and compact formulations of opposing beliefs in place, the evangelical interest in doctrinal correctness made a choice necessary. As we noted earlier, traditionalist evangelicals claimed the designation "evangelical" for their own and modernist evangelicals did nothing to stop them. This is how the modern split between evangelicals and liberals was born. Thus, the phrase "liberal evangelical" only became seemingly contradictory early in the twentieth century.

Second, though conservative evangelicals were heavily influenced by Fundamentalists, they were also much more diverse than Fundamentalists. They included the student movements mentioned above, for example. Fundamentalists attacked evangelicals for not being sufficiently concerned about doctrinal purity, for being too open to pietism and religious experience, and for consorting with the enemy in the form of ecumenical dialogues with moderates and liberals and cooperating with them on church mission projects. Fundamentalists increasingly tended to be separatists, wanting to withdraw from the apostate church into a "pure" church, and they chastised other evangelicals for not coming with them. For their part, most evangelicals simply did not want to follow the separatist example of Fundamentalists. Evangelicals held their concern for doctrinal purity in balance with the concern for church unity because their first concern was always with the evangelical power of the Christian gospel.

Under these pressures, the conservative evangelical block within Christianity in the United States broke apart fairly quickly. Most important, the moderate neo-evangelical movement emerged in the second quarter of the twentieth century as an articulate response to attacks from Fundamentalists. Once the dispute was thematized, it turned out to be about conflicting social strategies for the church to engage its cultural environment, just as we discussed toward the end of Part IV. Neo-evangelicals self-consciously positioned themselves between what they took to be militant Fundamentalist separatism and flaccid liberal accommodation. They kept the theology of the Fundamentals but argued for engaging culture and modern knowledge while maintaining a distinctively Christian identity rooted in biblical authority. Another motivation for neo-evangelicalism was the anti-intellectual character of Fundamentalism. Despite the rational bluster of Fundamentalists, many conservative evangelicals were embarrassed to be associated with them and so no longer wanted to use the originally noble term "fundamentalism" to describe themselves.

The name "neo-evangelical" was coined by well-known evangelical Harold Ockenga, cofounder of the influential

National Association of Evangelicals, as well as of Fuller and Gordon-Conwell seminaries. Ockenga used the term in a 1948 lecture. Later, reflecting on the event in his Foreword to Harold Lindsell's *The Battle for the Bible*, Ockenga wrote,

> Neo-evangelicalism was born in 1948 in connection with a convocation address which I gave in the Civic Auditorium in Pasadena. While reaffirming the theological view of fundamentalism, this address repudiated its ecclesiology and its social theory. The ringing call for a repudiation of separatism and the summons to social involvement received a hearty response from many evangelicals. The name caught on and spokesmen such as Drs. Harold Lindsell, Carl F.H. Henry, Edward Carnell, and Gleason Archer supported this viewpoint. We had no intention of launching a movement, but found that the emphasis attracted widespread support and exercised great influence. . . . Neo-evangelicals emphasized the restatement of Christian theology in accordance with the need of the times, the reengagement in the theological debate, the recapture of denominational leadership, and the reexamination of theological problems such as the antiquity of man, the universality of the flood, and God's method of creation.

The positive influence of the neo-evangelical movement is measured by the 1956 birth of what amounts to its flagship publication, the important periodical *Christianity Today*, founded by evangelist Billy Graham and first edited by evangelical theologian Carl Henry. Shockingly, Henry was eventually removed by the board because he insisted on fair representation of opponents' viewpoints in the magazine as a matter of intellectual honesty and moral responsibility, whereas the board wanted the magazine to portray a single line without any such complications. The magazine is better balanced today, but the controversy is indicative of the struggles between neo-evangelicals and conservative evangelicals at that time.

In fact, the neo-evangelical movement was relentlessly criticized by conservative evangelicals, and especially Fundamentalists, for compromising the fundamentals despite rhetoric to the contrary. Fundamentalists argued it was impossible to engage in the theological dialogue of the day and maintain biblical inerrancy in any meaningful sense. The Fundamentalists were correct about this, of course, just as they were correct all along about the decisiveness of the modernist-traditionalist debate. Neo-evangelicals did in fact surrender biblical inerrancy in the Fundamentalist sense, though they retained plenary inspiration of the Bible, in the sense that the whole is God-breathed. We, of course, think the neo-evangelicals made an excellent move.

Neo-evangelicalism has become a term of art that almost all evangelicals use to describe evangelical Christians who lie to their left on the liberal-conservative spectrum. It has a thousand meanings, accordingly. We have avoided the term in this book, but we have used the term "moderate evangelicals" to indicate the large number of evangelicals who stand today roughly for what many neo-evangelicals stood for in the mid-twentieth century. Some of those moderates are intensely interested in liberal evangelicalism, even though few of them have a name for it.

MODERN LIBERALISM

The history of modern evangelicalism is more spectacular than that of modern liberalism. This is because modern evangelicals have been fighting with each other from their very beginnings. Liberals have had really only one major fight, and that was the original modernist-traditionalist controversy. This controversy was born with biblical criticism, historical consciousness, and the deepening scientific view of the world. It heated up through the nineteenth century and exploded at the beginning of the twentieth century with the emergence of Fundamentalism. This extended battle over the truth defines the thematic heart of liberal Christianity and has direct implications for how they believe the church should engage its surrounding culture. We sketch that story here.

Modern liberal Christianity was born not in revivals but in influential congregational preacher-scholars such as Phillips Brooks (1835–1893), Washington Gladden (1836–1918), Russell

H. Conwell (1843–1925), and others with large urban congregations. It also owes something to universities, including especially
substreams within some of the evangelical student movements
mentioned earlier. Historically speaking, modern liberal Christianity includes that branch of evangelical Christianity willing
to consider favorably the determinations of historians and sci-
entists about what happened in the far past and how the world
works. This makes its authority structure profoundly different
than that of Christians who vest absolute authority in the Bible
or in ecclesiastical hierarchies.

For the liberal Christian, authority derives from many
sources simultaneously—Bible, reason, experience, tradition.
The spiritual challenge for the liberal Christian is striving for artful equilibration among the many aspects of knowledge and experience relevant to an intellectually responsible Christian faith.
This is utterly consistent with the early history of liberalism that
we sketched above: the individual must strive to integrate all relevant factors into a harmonious whole, taking responsibility for
his or her decisions along the way.

German theologian Friedrich Schleiermacher (1768–1834)
is sometimes called the father of liberal theology. A polymath,
Schleiermacher helped to found the Friedrich Wilhelm University in Berlin and was deeply involved in the union of Reformed
and Lutheran churches in Prussia. He was a devoted pastor and
a renowned preacher, he made the classic translation of Plato's
writings into German, he more or less founded the discipline of
hermeneutics, he gave birth to an existentialist and romantic approach to theology, and he wrote prodigiously as a theologian
and philosopher.

Among Schleiermacher's writings is a massively influential
systematic theology, translated in English as *The Christian Faith*.
This book does not talk much about God or the divine nature. In
fact, Schleiermacher said that if the times were more propitious,
he would have written a theology in which God was spoken of
as nothing more and nothing less than the source of the human
experience of absolute dependence. To him, the divine nature
necessarily surpassed the power of human comprehension, and
theologians ought to do more than just pay lip service to that fact.

Schleiermacher set the standard for taking seriously the heritage of the Christian faith, biblical criticism, historical consciousness, modern science, and cutting-edge philosophy simultaneously. In doing so he inspired many theologians in the liberal tradition.

Later in the nineteenth century, the international movement known as liberal Protestantism emerged. This movement became definitive of modernism in Christianity and the lightning rod for traditionalist attacks. In fact, liberal Protestantism was rather diverse, and predictably caricatured by its opponents in terms of its left most proponents. Among these was German historian and theologian Adolf von Harnack (1851–1930). Staggeringly prodigious as a historian, Harnack was best known among the general public for his best seller, *The Essence of Christianity*. Published in numerous languages almost immediately upon its appearance, and appearing in English in 1901, this book was enormously popular and defined the meaning of liberal Protestantism for many people.

Against other liberal intellectuals who were the historical skeptics of his era, Harnack believed that careful historical work could recover the essence of Jesus' teaching. That essence could be used to critique later developments in Christianity and prune Christian doctrine back to what was essential, eliminating distorting accretions. And what was the essence of the Christian gospel? It was a simple but potent moral message with three interpenetrating affirmations:

- the Kingdom of God and its coming,
- God the Father and the infinite value of the human soul, and
- the higher righteousness and the commandment of love

Harnack thought Jesus was neither a social reformer nor a political revolutionary but rather a teacher and example whose knowledge of God as Father is the full meaning of his identity as God's Son.

Liberal theologians took historical criticism for granted. It is important to grasp that so-called higher criticism was typically not problematic for them. If they grew up in a highly traditional background, liberal theologians typically embraced historical-critical approaches to the Bible with relief, as an escape from an impossibly contorted and implausible world of biblical interpretation and doctrinal rationalization. Historical criticism was liberating for their faith, a source of great strength and comfort, and compelling evidence that Christianity could be as intellectually robust as anything in the world of human thought. Fundamentalists find this appalling, and some conservative Christians may find it difficult to grasp. It is true nonetheless.

At the beginning of the twentieth century, liberal Protestantism in the United States developed in four basic directions partly in response to the traditionalist-modernist debate and partly due to intrinsic intellectual pressures. These were friendly divergences involving none of the bitter fighting that conservative evangelicals had to endure during the same period.

First, a liberal form of evangelicalism emerged, or perhaps an evangelical form of liberalism, depending on how you tell the story. We will talk further about that, because this marks the origins of the liberal-evangelical tradition we wish to nurture in a new form in our own time. The important point here is that it has roots equally strong in late-nineteenth-century evangelicalism and late-nineteenth-century liberalism.

Second, the Transcendentalism of Ralph Waldo Emerson (1803–1882), Theodore Parker (1810–1860), and others emerged in the New England area. A distinctively American development, Transcendentalism evolved from American Unitarianism, an older form of liberal Christianity. It eventually became the dominant form of American Unitarianism, which typically retained only weak links to its Christian origins.

Third, a kind of philosophical theology developed around the University of Chicago. Known as the Chicago School, or American Modernism, it was far more radical than liberal evangelicalism, emphasizing empiricism in theology, exploring naturalistic worldviews, and sometimes dramatically reframing Christian doctrines. It became the fertile bed for the seed of process theology when it arrived later in midcentury. Some of the key figures in the Chicago School are Shailer Matthews (1863–1941), Douglas Clyde Macintosh (1877–1948), and Henry Nelson Wieman (1884–1975).

Finally, liberal Protestantism's best-known American child is the Social Gospel movement, associated especially with Walter Rauschenbusch (1861–1918). This movement conveyed to liberal Christianity the passionate evangelical commitment to social justice and confirmed its suspicion of all human economic and social arrangements—emphases that are fully evident still today.

The historic importance of the Social Gospel lies in the fact that it made a difference to ordinary people at a time when the churches experienced moral paralysis in the face of the economic changes of the industrial revolution. The end of the nineteenth century utterly transformed the meaning of work—roughly, work changed from outdoors to factories, handwork to machine-work, creativity to repetition, self-direction to loss of autonomy, and so on. Workers launched bloody strikes in an attempt to get the wealthy drivers of the American industrial revolution to pay attention to their plight.

Meanwhile, the church unthinkingly supported the sort of laissez-faire economic policies that supposed God fitted each person to his or her fate, and everyone just had to accept this. Factory workers should just buckle down and do what they are told. This lack of perception by the churches was challenged by the roughly simultaneous emergence of the trade union movement, the Social Gospel movement, and the Salvation Army. Only later did the churches catch on, led by Pope Leo XIII's encyclical *Rerum Novarum* and the liberal and mainline denominations.

CHAPTER 14

Liberal Evangelicalism

We now take up the distinctive history of the early liberal-evangelical movement, which arose in the same period as the great evangelical split that established a sharp contrast between liberal and conservative forms of evangelical Christianity.

A History All Its Own

We explained in the previous chapter how, over a century ago, Protestant evangelicals were alarmed to discover a conservative-liberal division in their ranks, which they thought of in terms of traditionalism versus modernism. The two sides held much in common, particularly their passion for evangelism and fervent faith, and yet the difference was unmistakable.

The liberals among the evangelicals saw the plausibility of the gospel—both its beliefs and the resulting lifestyles and social action—as the key to attracting a new generation of souls to the Christian Way. They did not accept inerrancy of the Bible and flourished in the cultural world of ideas, honoring the Bible while savoring literature, historical criticism, and science. Meanwhile, the conservatives among the evangelicals trusted in the authority of established wisdom for winning converts and so cleaved to traditional ways of expressing Christian faith. They held fast to the fundamentals and feared their liberal brethren were selling the Christian birthright for a bowl of pottage.

Both sides in the evangelical split tended to believe that the progress of human civilization and technology were signs of God's blessing—that was a North American cultural conviction as much as anything. Liberal evangelicals were initially more enthusiastic and conservative evangelicals more wary about this, though in due course this polarity would reverse. More consistent from then until now has been another correlation: evangelicals affirming postmillennialism, involving the gradual perfection of society, tended to be liberal, while those affirming premillennialism, involving the degeneration of society and apostasy of the church, tended to be conservative. Of course, there were exceptions, as well as evangelicals of both sorts who weren't sure.

We are especially interested in the moderates of the era of the great evangelical split. There were many of them in ordinary churches and in the evangelical student movements. The liberals or modernists of the nineteenth century went in many directions, but only the moderates among them made a strong effort to remain true to all sides of their evangelical heritage. Likewise, the conservatives or traditionalists of the nineteenth century could not hold together because evangelicalism's double interest in doctrinal purity and the unity of the Christian witness proved to be explosively incompatible.

In our analysis, the Fundamentalists overstressed purity of doctrine and church, criticized everyone who was not exactly like them, drove moderate evangelicals away, and then shattered into a thousand pieces under internal disagreements. They are now left with an unappetizing struggle. They have to distinguish themselves from the dangerous forms of anti-intellectual Fundamentalism evident in all modern religions—movements that stress absolute external authority and purity of doctrine and practice, just like Christian Fundamentalists. But this is a predictable outcome of abandoning evangelical Christianity's classic balance of clear Christian identity and unified Christian witness.

In the same way, the liberals who lost track of the centrality of Jesus Christ in their explorations of worlds beyond the Bible abandoned their Christian roots or created Unitarian churches that are typically uncomfortable with their own Christian heritage. Neither the post-Christians nor the Unitarians, nor the anti-ecumenical separatist Fundamentalists, feel that anything has gone wrong, except possibly with everyone else. We have no serious hope that the ideals of liberal-evangelical faith can influence them. From the moderate perspective, they all went too far.

On the conservative side of the great evangelical split, moderates were at first enthusiastic about the fundamentalist reform and wore the fundamentalist label like a badge of honor. They quickly recognized its lack of balance, however, and tried to reclaim the prized evangelical balance, eventually defining themselves as neo-evangelicals. On the liberal side of the great split, moderates were watching the chaos among conservatives from the outside, because the liberal rejection of biblical inerrancy made them persona non grata. Yet they held fast to their evangelicalism, in the classically balanced nineteenth-century sense that we have described. In particular, they resisted the loss of Christ-centeredness among their liberal brethren, who really had no interest in remaining evangelical in any sense. These liberal evangelicals were the last evangelicals standing on the liberal side of the great split, as all of the other liberals gladly abandoned the "evangelical" label. But the liberal evangelicals were a sizable group and included many in the mainline denominations. This group of liberal evangelicals immediately recognized serious allies among the neo-evangelical resistance to the Fundamentalist betrayal of classical evangelicalism.

These two families of moderate evangelicals did not just sit still and watch the liberal-conservative cultural and theological split destroy their vision of a church united under the banner of the gospel of Jesus Christ. It is easy to forget this in an era when the religious airwaves are dominated by conservative evangelicals and Fundamentalists and when populist political liberals often do not take religion seriously because of its shrill conservative representatives. Yet those early moderates began dialogues between the liberal and neo-evangelical wings of evangelicalism, some of which continue to this day. This group of moderates, some of whom we discuss below, still tries to hold the ecumenical line of evangelical Christian unity against the fearsome onslaught of culture wars and theological diversity. These efforts remind us that the trumpet call to Christian unity under the evangelical banner is not forgotten, even if it has become a faint cry rather than the penetrating sound of earlier generations.

Despite the efforts to keep moderate evangelical Protestant Christianity together, any honest historian has to admit frankly that the ideal of evangelical unity has failed—not utterly, to be sure, but significantly. Perhaps this was inevitable. Church splits may be the only way to handle the stress of ideological and theological pluralism when it becomes extreme. Splitting is better than warring. Arguably, the liberal versus conservative ideological split, with its moral and theological correlations, was always going to be too much for evangelical Christianity to accommodate. Reuniting liberal evangelicals and conservative evangelicals anywhere except over the dialogue table would probably be a disaster because of their blunt disagreement over biblical inerrancy and the role of external authority in authentic Christian identity. It is better to allow them to cultivate the subcultural identity of being embattled and thriving, as discussed at the end of Part IV. We have no interest in urging liberal and conservative Christians to reunite, though we fiercely protest hostility and proclaim the minimalist cultural virtue of courtesy now that the more adventurous ideal of Christian unity has failed.

We are more worried about a devastating side effect of the great evangelical split for the identity of Christian moderates. Conservatives claimed the word "evangelical," and it now appears that only conservatives can be evangelical; liberals have to be something else or just go away. Here we see at work that element of the history of evangelicalism that defines subcultural identity through naming an enemy. In this case, the enemy is liberalism, formerly modernism, with its acceptance of biblical criticism, historical consciousness, modern science, and a balanced approach to authority. Conservative evangelicals see themselves as the true remnant of Christianity, proclaiming the gospel when everyone else, especially the liberal church, has forsaken the truth.

Based on everything we have said about the history of the words and the movements of liberalism and evangelicalism, we conclude that this is aggressive semantic theft. The split between liberals and conservatives happened in many places in Western civilization. To the extent that it happened within evangelical Protestantism, both severed wings of the movement have a rightful claim to call themselves evangelicals.

Sadly, the moderates for whom we write this book typically know nothing about this early history of liberal evangelicalism and feel out of place or, as we call it, lost in the middle. The liberals who follow Jesus Christ are passionate Christians in exactly the balanced way of classical evangelicalism before the great split that changed the meaning of the word "evangelical," but most have never heard of their liberal-evangelical forebears. Many neo-evangelicals uncomfortable with the shrill implausibility of biblical inerrancy also know nothing about the liberal-evangelical history and feel alienated in their evangelical context. We think each of these groups would be greatly helped to know more about their own heritage. This knowledge will help them establish an identity as moderates who cleave to classical evangelical ideals: Christ-centered Christian identity, unity of Christian witness, evangelical fervor, and social action.

It is worth noting the parallels to this complex history beyond the limits of Protestantism in the Western world. Catholic Christianity systematically suppressed its liberal wing, which was also designated "modernism." Apart from tolerant havens of some monastic orders and the Second Vatican Council, variously regarded as a breath of fresh air or a devastating mistake, the Catholic Church's hierarchy stayed locked in a conservative posture for most of the twentieth century. Meanwhile, European colonialism and the accompanying Protestant and Catholic mission movements bore fruit to the point that Christians outside the North Atlantic world are now more numerous than those within. The face of global Christianity has changed dramatically. It is conservative forms of Catholic and evangelical Protestant Christianity that have caught on in most places. But all over the world minority liberal impulses toward flexibility and reform in doctrine and practice have sprung up. Typically these are the result of indigenous theological and ecclesial responses to local challenges and seek to reassert cultural authenticity against the ravages of colonialism. In the world of postcolonial Christianity, liberal-evangelical moderation has a great deal to offer.

LIBERAL-EVANGELICAL HEROES

The complementarity between liberalism and evangelicalism that many moderates of our own time intuitively sense is more than merely possible. It has been and is now a reality. One way to grasp this is to consider examples of liberal-evangelical church leaders.

Within the United States, the liberal evangelicals have been centrally inspired by figures such as William Newton Clarke (1841–1912), Walter Rauschenbusch (1861–1918), Henry Churchill King (1858–1934), William Adams Brown (1865–1943), and the "Billy Graham of India," E. Stanley Jones (1884–1973). These intellectuals and churchmen sought to articulate a Christian theology that would have evangelical potency for modern people. Such a theology needed to take biblical criticism, historical consciousness, modern science, and religious pluralism with the utmost seriousness. But it also needed to remain Christ-centered and to retain the Bible as a meaningful authority for Christian belief and practice. Like the liberal Protestants, the liberal-evangelical movement was skeptical of metaphysically articulated doctrines as overreaching human rational capabilities. Liberal evangelicals tended to be strongly concerned with social conditions and always led the way within the denominational contexts in sparking the moral conscience of the church.

The founding father of liberal evangelicalism was probably Horace Bushnell (1802–1876) as much as anyone. He died a full generation prior to the great evangelical split but was deeply sensitive to the brewing conflict between modernists and traditionalists and indeed was right in the middle of it in his own day. Bushnell was pastor of the North Congregational Church in Hartford, Connecticut, from 1833 to 1859. He was an active author and prodigiously influential in the American religious scene. He argued against the rigid Calvinistic orthodoxy of his day, a specter of doctrinal turgidity that would have puzzled Calvin himself, and in favor of a simple theology that ordinary people could understand. He urged Christians to recognize that God's mystery surpasses human understanding and that we can never hope for a fully adequate dogmatic theology. Rather, we have to tell the story of God's relationship to humanity more in the way that Jesus did, plainly, with room for growing awareness in each life and sensitivity to deepening historical knowledge. His Christ-centeredness and evangelical passion were unmistakable, and he led a courageous life at the intersection of those great evangelical convictions.

In the time after the great evangelical split, the archetypal liberal evangelical was probably the renowned preacher Harry Emerson Fosdick (1878–1969). A passionate evangelist, Fosdick was one of the great preachers of the twentieth century. For almost two decades, he maintained an international Christian radio program called *National Vespers Hour* that made him the most listened-to preacher in human history up until that time. He was a Baptist but served as associate pastor of First Presbyterian Church in New York City (1918-1924), and then as senior pastor of Park Avenue Baptist Church, which ultimately became, under his leadership, the famous interdenominational Riverside Church. He taught at the adjacent Union Theological Seminary from 1908 to 1946 and held a professorial appointment there in practical theology from 1915 to 1934.

Fosdick was a prodigious author with fifty books and hundreds of articles. He was deeply embedded in the great events of the day throughout his life, warmly connected to leading national political figures, a trustee at the Rockefeller Foundation, and rightly dubbed "the Senior Pastor of the American Establishment." This role would later fall to neo-evangelical Billy Graham, whose simple, honest theology and evangelical passion closely resembled that of Fosdick. The general public would have regarded Fosdick as liberal and Graham as conservative, but this merely illustrates the difficulty of naming moderate evangelicals in the era after the great split.

Fosdick explicitly described himself as a liberal evangelical. As a mature Christian, he stressed Christ-centeredness, humility in doctrine, unity of the church's witness, and the accessibility of theology to ordinary Christians. But he had a difficult journey reaching the powerful theological position he eventually inhabited. His personal struggle against the constricting Calvinism of his day was intense. He could not fathom how the God he loved could consign human beings to eternal punishment in the flames of hell before they were even born. Despairing of happiness and integrity, he attempted suicide in 1902 as a young seminarian. After that defining event, Fosdick seemed somehow freed from the oppressive doctrinal rigidity of his background and forged a new way of speaking about his faith. He graduated with superior grades from Union Theological Seminary and went on to revitalize liberal evangelical rhetoric, using his powerful oratory to defend moderate Christianity from its conservative and secular liberal detractors alike.

As an example, well-intentioned Fundamentalist William Jennings Bryan, the successful lawyer of Scopes Monkey Trial fame, aggressively attacked Fosdick in 1922. Fosdick's reply was a sermon entitled "Shall the Fundamentalists Win?" that propelled him into national prominence. Ordinary American Christians observed his articulate and compelling defense of a moderate form of Christianity that joined passion with tolerance, and many were deeply impressed. In fact, Fosdick's reply to Bryan probably did more than any other single event to consolidate the word "Fundamentalist" in the American vocabulary, even while critiquing it.

We could mention more of our liberal-evangelical heroes, such as German anti-Hitler theologian Dietrich Bonhoeffer, the Niebuhr brothers Reinhold and Richard, Howard Thurman, Martin Luther King Jr., Barbara Brown Taylor, and Bishop John Shelby Spong. But we have said enough. The currently sharp tension between "liberal" and "evangelical" is atypical of the history of these words and the ideas they express. *The liberal urge toward humble openness and the evangelical impulse toward passionate commitment are not alien to one another.* Past eras show us they were united and even suggest how we might put them together again in our own time.

A Moderate Conclusion

If you are a moderate Christian of the liberal-evangelical type, how might the historical information in the chapters of Part V affect your self-understanding? What can you do, practically and positively, about this new self-understanding?

Regarding self-understanding, if you are a moderate Christian, you may sometimes feel like a spiritual nomad without a family, longing to know your own ancestors. The good news is that you have a heritage. It is a noble heritage, intellectually profound and authentically Christian. Fundamentalists hate it for its moderation, its radical inclusiveness, its social engagement, and its refusal to prioritize doctrinal purity over the ecumenical unity of Christian witness. Secular liberals have little sympathy for its authentic Christ-centeredness and its refusal to abandon traditional claims about the centrality of God in creation. People seem to have forgotten Fosdick's self-designation as a liberal evangelical. This is not surprising, given the semantic shifts in the meanings of these terms after the great evangelical split. But it is a great tragedy that moderate Christians of our own day are cut off from this liberal-evangelical heritage. This is the location of their spiritual ancestors and where they can learn to feel at home themselves.

Regarding action, if you are a moderate Christian learning about your spiritual ancestry for the first time, consider how you would react to learning about your biological family heritage. You may well choose to try to get to know your grandparents and great-grandparents as well as you can. In the same way, you could choose to read about your liberal-evangelical ancestors, collect their photographs, or perhaps read some of what they wrote or preached. A good starting point for studying your spiritual family tree is the resources section of the LiberalEvangelical.org website. But don't stop there. As you read and learn more, find your own liberal-evangelical hero and make a point of getting on the inside of his or her way of feeling and thinking. These people had—and have—remarkably integrated intellectual and spiritual perspectives. There is enormous profit in understanding how they wove the various threads of their lives together into the beautiful, complex tapestries that we celebrate today.

Conclusion

In this conclusion, we first review the argument of this book, part by part. Subsequently, we will reflect on the value of what we have presented both for changing the self-understanding of moderate Christians with liberal and evangelical instincts and for discerning next steps in individual faith journeys and church communities.

REVIEW

Part I reflected on the personal meaning for moderate Christians with a liberal-evangelical faith identity. In Chapter 1 we discussed a number of existential questions that thoughtful Christian people tend to have. Christian theological subcultures offer quite different answers to such questions, often firmly attached to the labels "liberal" and "evangelical." That leaves moderates often feeling lost in the middle, as well as frustrated and neglected. Beneath these different answers are serious disagreements. In Chapter 2 we drew five of these disagreements into the open.

- Conflicting visions of reality involve a clash between colorful *supernaturalistic* views of the world, complete with miracles and discarnate entities such as demons and angels, and deeply spiritual but *naturalistic* visions of reality in which God is the mystery and depth of the glorious natural world.

- Conflicting visions of authority involve a clash between the *definitive-authority* view that prizes certainty and vests authority in a miraculously created Bible and the *tradition-authority* view in which vast traditions explore religious realities, accruing wisdom in the Bible and elsewhere, and slowly mutating in the process.
- Conflicting visions of history involve a clash between a *crisis* view in which human civilization can't perfect itself but must be destroyed, judged, and re-created by God and a *developmental* view in which God's perfecting grace is demonstrated in the growth of technologies that alleviate suffering and enrich human life.
- Conflicting visions of morality involve a clash between a *thickly-textured morality* in which all moral intuitions are God-given and should be without reservation and a *thinly-textured morality* in which moral intuitions about fairness and compassion are God-given, while moral intuitions about in-group loyalty, hierarchy, and purity are heavily suspect because they lead to exclusion and persecution.
- Finally, conflicting visions of church involve a clash between an ecclesiological ideal of *purity* of doctrine and worship and an ecclesiological ideal of *inclusiveness*, which is modeled after Jesus' radically inclusive ministry, as recalled and recorded in the New Testament gospels.

We argued that getting beyond one-sided liberal and one-sided evangelical answers requires understanding these disagreements clearly and then choosing to remain connected to faith with your eyes wide open to what is involved in worshiping and serving alongside others who may think differently than you do.

Part II laid out the problem and promise of a moderate Christian identity. We described political and religious moderates with the aid of demographic data in Chapter 3. We discovered moderates are in the majority on both the political and religious spectrums, and there is a resurgence of interest in moderate politics and faith. In Chapter 4 we discussed the way contemporary culture wars ratchet up tension between the religious extremes, leaving moderates feeling lost in the middle. There they witness the extremes caricaturing and attacking one another, while moderates find themselves appreciating some elements of both wings. In Chapter 5 we discussed reasons for the reassertion of a more self-conscious form of Christian unity, which we call liberal-evangelical Christianity.

Part III discussed the way that political and social tensions are entangled with the liberal versus evangelical religious conflict. In Chapter 6 we analyzed the reasons for political conflict and polarization and made an attempt to name what it is about political liberals and political conservatives that they most want to nurture and protect. We argued that moderates instinctively grasp the valuable heart of both extremes. In Chapter 7 we described the two-way interaction between religion and politics and how political and religious polarizations reinforce and exacerbate one another. We also described moderate resistance that deconstructs the polarization in religion and politics and refocuses attention on common values and vital shared interests. This resistance to polarized extremes is the secret of liberal-evangelical Christianity's transformative contribution to cultural life; it is a potentially revolutionary witness to the power of love. In Chapter 8 we analyzed styles of moral reasoning that explain why the extremes of the political and religious spectrums have characteristic moral convictions and demands. This is one of several parts of the book that is closely associated with the history and politics of the United States. But many of the dynamics we discussed have parallels in other national contexts. Moderate Christians in other countries will have their own versions of the story of institutional expectations, church-state relations, and moral reasoning styles that we recount for the U.S. context.

Part IV dug into the sociology of the liberal versus evangelical conflict. In Chapter 9 we presented basic sociological principles that explain group behavior such as the clustering of like-minded people, the negative side effects of such comfortable clustering behaviors, and the paralyzing threat of excessive pluralism around group identity issues. Chapter 10 presented the fundamental reason that pluralism of theology and ethics arises within Christianity. We called this *core message pluralism*, which is the presence of more than one way of seeing the Christian message right at the heart of its founding documents and traditions. We laid out the resulting mismatch between evangelical and liberal gospels. Liberal Christianity and evangelical Christianity represent opposed strategies for managing core message pluralism. Both strategies are intelligent in that they minimize the socially demanding need for unity in the face of diverse beliefs and practices, though one is currently more successful than the other. In Chapter 11 we discussed the various social strategies that Christian and non-Christian groups use to navigate the challenge of diversity of belief and practice. We discussed why the liberal-evangelical form of moderate Christianity must fly in the face of convention, defying sociological probabilities, to forge loving unity in the face of significant differences in belief and practice— a truly countercultural ideal. We argued that this is a demanding spiritual and ecclesial path but one with impeccable biblical and ecumenical credentials.

Part V showed that the liberal-evangelical option for moderate Christian faith is not a novel one. In fact, it is a retrieval of a longstanding possibility within Protestant Christianity, drawing on classic insights from the longer and broader Christian tradition. Chapter 12 sketched the early histories of evangelical Christianity and liberal Christianity, and Chapter 13 outlined the modern history of liberalism and evangelicalism. We described how the liberal-conservative split arose within evangelical Christianity early in the twentieth century, the semantic theft of the word "evangelical" by conservatives, and the docile surrender of the word by liberals. This history retrieves wonderful dimensions of meaning in the words "liberal" and "evangelical" that Christians of most kinds, and certainly moderates, can appreciate. In Chapter 14 we sketched the distinctive history of liberal-evangelical Christianity, including inspiring examples of church leaders who were simultaneously liberal and evangelical. We argued that knowledge of history can point the way to new possibilities for people mired in the conflicts of the present.

TRANSFORMING SELF-UNDERSTANDING, DISCERNING NEXT STEPS

In this book we have tried to help you, our moderate readers with liberal and evangelical instincts, grasp your situation. You may be a pastor, a seminary student, a lay leader, or a thoughtful Christian layperson. For each of you, getting oriented to your moderate situation involves recognizing a phenomenon, diagnosing a problem with it, and discovering the promise within it.

The *phenomenon* is the emergence (or reemergence) of a moderate form of Christianity that seems neither exclusively liberal nor exclusively evangelical but in some ways both at once. Unlike the coordinated planning associated with neo-evangelicalism, as it distinguished itself in the 1950s from fundamentalism, the liberal-evangelical phenomenon is a barely noticed migration, motivated by dissatisfaction with polarized extremes in religion and politics. It overlaps with the so-called emergent church and the Christian practices movements but is more diffuse and more inclusive than these movements. It currently lacks support from theologians and religious leaders, which makes it a confusing location from which to build a clear and coherent Christian identity. Yet this moderate migration is a quietly growing reality because of the appeal of the classic balance of liberal and evangelical virtues that it represents.

The *problem* is that "liberal" and "evangelical" seem to be opposed categories, which makes it additionally difficult to grasp this phenomenon and leaves moderate Christians like you without the terminology and support you need to articulate your identity. We have argued that "liberal" and "evangelical" can be complementary categories when interpreted properly. These terms should be pressed into service to understand the renewal of moderate Christianity in our time and to create conceptual and social space for the reassertion of a liberal-evangelical form of moderate Christianity.

The *promise* of this form of moderate Christianity is the opportunity it presents for you and other moderates like you to demonstrate a potently countercultural form of social organization—ordinary people bound by love despite significant differences in theological, moral, and political convictions. This flies in the face of a culture that readily accommodates and customizes its social structures to the special interests of its members. Seriously disagreeing in love has become an utterly lost art. This liberal-evangelical form of moderate Christianity is passionate about a church that swims upstream against the cultural current, that defies sociological probabilities to portray a transformative possibility for human communities, and that demands lifestyles of radical discipleship, devoted study, and compassionate social engagement.

This possibility of loving unity in difference becomes increasingly vital with every passing year as the texture of communities steadily reduces dangerously close to the bare minimum, which is (to put it bluntly) the sort of economic cooperation and semi-civil public discourse needed to avoid civil war. It just makes sense to most people to clump with others like them, to reduce the feelings of discomfort that pluralism brings. Yet the Christians we have been addressing, moderates such as you, are suspicious of the simplicity of social clumping and the resulting polarization and seek to inhabit the difficult middle. *In the middle, spiritual maturity and wisdom are necessary for unity; like-mindedness is not enough.*

People drop off to the left and right whenever the task of achieving unity under these circumstances proves too difficult. For instance, people who reject the liberal-evangelical ideal of taking the Bible seriously but not always literally may not be able to cope with sermons and Bible studies that embrace cutting-edge historical and literary study of the scriptures. People for whom Christ-centered discipleship is unappealing may find the liberal-evangelical community an uncongenial place, despite feeling accepted there. So there are limits to the diversity that liberal-evangelical congregations can tolerate, and some people will migrate away from the middle. But—and this is crucial—others constantly migrate to the center from the outer edges. Like you, they are suspicious of the ideological narrowness of their more extreme church worlds, and they seek a better-grounded faith in a well-rounded community of Christian disciples. The social strategy for survival and unity in the liberal-evangelical church is a curious one. Yet it is also potentially effective in our context because it is a crucial witness to the power of love in an era of relentless culture wars.

The five parts of this book offered complementary perspectives on the phenomenon, problem, and promise of Christians with both liberal and evangelical instincts. We hope that each part has helped you enhance your *self-understanding* and discern *practical and positive next steps* that work for you.

Regarding self-understanding, we hope you learned something about why being a moderate Christian with both liberal and evangelical instincts can be extremely uncomfortable in our time and place. Through demographic, historical, political, ethical, sociological, and theological reflections, we have explained how this situation developed and diagnosed its underlying social dynamics. We hope you recognized yourself in these reflections, found new resources for self-understanding, and discovered a rising satisfaction with your moderate faith location.

Regarding practical and positive next steps, we have two hopes. On the one hand, we hope you feel better able to take a chance and *speak out* using these new resources for talking about who you are, what you value, and how you want to act in the polarized contemporary Christian environment. We know that speaking out, even tentatively, is not easy at first. Applying new self-understandings in everyday life requires practice. So be patient with yourself. Start with describing your moderate faith with people you trust. As you gently try on the new self-understanding of yourself as a moderate committed to Christ-centered radical inclusivism, you can expect to see changes. Your confidence will grow. There is nothing quite as rewarding as finally finding the ideas that allow you to speak clearly about the convictions you have held all along. Also, those with whom you speak may also come to feel more spiritually oriented and come to share your excitement. Even when people flatly disagree with you, you can feel your convictions settling into place and becoming more persuasive and better articulated.

On the other hand, we hope you feel better able to discern how to put your faith into practice. The resources we have presented establish principles for creative action, such as empathy for the Other, radical inclusiveness, Christ-centeredness, and diligent study to increase awareness and perception of the political and religious worlds you inhabit. It makes sense that gaining the ability to describe your conflicted experience articulately is the first step toward building a tool kit for practical decision making. It is quite interesting to monitor the way that your ability to construct plans of action deepens as you become more articulate in your radically moderate faith. For example, once you realize that you stand for Christ-centered inclusivism, inspired by the New Testament's records of Jesus' own life and ministry, your decisions about how to treat strangers or people who are different from you can shift quite dramatically. That can quickly transform the way you think about the social work of your church or the way one is invited to Holy Communion.

At several places in this book, we spoke about the threefold challenge of radical discipleship, devoted study, and compassionate social engagement.

- The commitment to radical discipleship involves a Christ-centered spirituality that impacts everything from your beliefs to your behavior. A good way to enhance your discipleship is to meditate on the life of Jesus, guided by the biblical accounts of his actions and teachings.
- The commitment to devoted study arises from the fact that your situation in contemporary Christian debates is a nuanced but potent one and demands that you work hard to become articulate about it. A good way to enhance your learning is to find a group with whom you can study this book or its companion volume on theology and ethics, *Found in the Middle!*, perhaps using the study guides provided on LiberalEvangelical.org.
- The commitment to compassionate social engagement goes hand in hand with inclusiveness: your calling as an individual Christian is to love those who Jesus loved. A good place to start there is to ponder how radical inclusiveness is manifested, or could be manifested, in your own life and in your local church community.

At the community level, new ideas need discussion to be properly absorbed and evaluated. For concrete advice about programs that moderate Christians and churches can embrace, turn to the literature surrounding the emergent church movement and the religious practices movement. Good examples of such resources are Diana Butler Bass, *Christianity for the Rest of Us* and *The Practicing Congregation*; Gil Rendle and Alice Mann, *Holy Conversations*; Anthony B. Robinson, *Transforming Congregational Culture* and *Leadership for Vital Congregations*; and a number of other books that are filled with concrete suggestions and well-tested advice. There is also the LiberalEvangelical.org website, which includes study guides, resources for liberal-evangelical Christians and congregations, and forums for discussing your faith and your church situation with others.

We know we are in an age when a vast swath of Christianity feels lost and ill at ease within the traditional theological confines of believing communities. As members of mainline denominations that are struggling to manage financially with an ever-decreasing membership base, we know that the church is feeling lost in a culture that is at best skeptical of our communities and at worst outright hostile to organized faith. We know that pastors look out at their troubled congregations week in and week out while wondering why something of the Pentecost experience of the early church doesn't just rush in and ignite the tired faith of those faithful warriors who attend week in and week out, giving themselves in service to Christ and the church.

Yet, we also know, beyond a shadow of a doubt, that a vital Christian faith, a vital Christian church, and vital Christian leadership are within our grasp. It may happen more subtly than rushing winds and tongues of fire, but we have witnessed and have come to believe that just this kind of vitality is breathed into church communities when Christians embrace the call to love liberally while sharing the gospel of Jesus Christ energetically. A liberal and evangelical movement is gaining momentum in churches and seminaries and within the hearts and minds of pastors throughout our country. Though there are huge numbers of Christians feeling lost in the middle of a liberal and conservative split within our religious landscape, we believe that those Christians are ready to be found by a movement of faith that welcomes them as they are and encourages them to follow Jesus as they are truly called. We are indeed lost in many ways, but we trust that, through the grace of God, we can always be found, right where we are, in the middle.

Resources for Further Study

PREFACE

There are many resources from the emergent church and religious practices movements that promise concrete advice to moderate Christians and church leaders about what to do in their lives and in their churches. In addition to those mentioned in the preface (details below), The Alban Institute (www.alban.org) carries a rich collection of relevant resources.

Diana Butler Bass, *Christianity for the Rest of Us: How the Neighborhood Church Is Transforming the Faith* (San Francisco: HarperOne, 2006).
———, *The Practicing Congregation: Imagining a New Old Church* (Herndon, VA: Alban Institute, 2004).
Gil Rendle and Alice Mann, *Holy Conversations: Strategic Planning as a Spiritual Practice for Congregations* (Herndon, VA: Alban Institute, 2003).
Anthony B. Robinson, *Leadership for Vital Congregations* (Cleveland: Pilgrim Press, 2007).
———, *Transforming Congregational Culture* (Grand Rapids, MI: Eerdmans Publishing Company, 2003).

PART I

Part I's existential perspective draws mostly on our own personal experience working with people in ministry and educational settings. A few books in this vein that are worth studying are:

John B. Cobb, *Becoming a Thinking Christian* (Nashville: Abingdon
    Press, 1993).

H. Richard Niebuhr, *Christ and Culture* (New York: Harper & Row,
    1951).

John A. T. Robinson, *Honest to God, Fortieth Anniversary Edition*
    (Louisville, KY: Westminster John Knox Press, 2006).

John Shelby Spong, *Rescuing the Bible from Fundamentalism:
    A Bishop Rethinks the Meaning of Scripture* (San Francisco:
    HarperOne, 1992).

Part II

Part II's demographic perspective analyzes survey data from
four principal sources. Each is accessible to the general public
and a good place to explore the issues further.

The Association of Religion Data Archives (www.thearda.com).
    This is a major repository of survey data pertinent to religion,
    politics, and Christian congregations.

The Barna Group (www.barna.org). See the "Barna by Topic" page
    and the "Recent Barna Updates" for the survey data reported
    here.

Baylor Institute for Studies of Religion, "American Piety in
    the 21st century" (September 2006) (www.isreligion.org).

The Pew Forum on Religion and Public Life (pewforum.org/
    religion–politics/). This site includes numerous resources
    for learning more about the complex relations between the
    religious and political spheres. See the "Surveys" page for the
    survey data reported here.

To find out more about the resurgence of Christian moderate
movements, visit the following publications and websites, paying particular attention to links to related organizations.

The Progressive Christian Witness. "A Web–based resource
    (www.progressivechristianwitness.org) that aims to
    strengthen the voices of progressive Christianity in the

public square by publishing theologically grounded articles for laypeople and pastors on significant issues in American life." In particular, for an introduction to other moderate movements, consult the "Other Voices" page.

Sojourners (www.sojo.org). "Founded in 1971, Sojourners is a Christian ministry whose mission is to proclaim and practice the biblical call to integrate spiritual renewal and social justice."

Some of the important books mentioned in Part II that are worth reading carefully include:

David Kuo, *Tempting Faith: An Inside Story of Political Seduction* (New York: Free Press, 2006).

Barack Obama, *The Audacity of Hope: Thoughts on Reclaiming the American Dream* (New York: Crown, 2006).

Jim Wallis, *God's Politics: Why the Right Gets It Wrong and the Left Doesn't Get It* (San Francisco: HarperOne, 2005).

Part III

Part III's political perspective draws on numerous sources, each of which is worth exploring.

Morris P. Florina, with Samuel J. Abrams and Jeremy C. Pope, *Culture War? The Myth of a Polarized America* (New York: Pearson Longman, 2004).

Edward Gibbon, *The History of the Decline and Fall of the Roman Empire*, 6 vols. (London: Straham, 1774–1778).

Jonathan Haidt (people.virginia.edu/~jdh6n/) includes summaries of his research and also selected writings that explain the material discussed in this chapter.

Laura Koenig and Thomas Bouchard, "Genetic and Environmental Influences on the Traditional Moral Values Triad—Authoritarianism, Conservatism and Religiousness— as Assessed by Quantitative Behavior Genetic Methods," in Patrick McNamara, ed., *Where God and Science Meet: How*

Brain and Evolutionary Studies Alter Our Understanding of Religion (3 vols.), vol. 1: *Evolution, Religion, and the Religious Brain* (Westport, CT: Praeger Publishers, 2006).

Reinhold Niebuhr, *Moral Man and Immoral Society* (New York and London: Charles Scribner's Sons, 1932).

Alexis de Tocqueville, *Democracy in America*, 2 vols., English translation of *De la Démocratie en Amérique* (London: Saunders and Otley, 1835–1840).

Robert Wuthnow, *The Struggle for America's Soul: Evangelicals, Liberals, and Secularism* (Grand Rapids, MI: Eerdmans, 1989).

The sources for surveys in this chapter not already mentioned are:

Lilly Endowment's 1987 Church and Community Project (www.thearda.com/Archive/Files/Descriptions/CCPI.asp).

The Pew Research Center's 2002 Religion and Public Life Survey (people–press.org/dataarchive/).

2006 Baylor Religion Survey (www.isreligion.org).

PART IV

Part IV's sociological perspective draws on a complex literature in the sociology of religion, which is gripping or alienating, depending on how you look at it. Good places to go for further study are:

Diana Butler Bass, *Christianity for the Rest of Us: How the Neighborhood Church Is Transforming the Faith* (San Francisco: HarperOne, 2006).

Peter L. Berger, *Sacred Canopy: A Sociological Theory of Religion* (New York: Anchor Books, 1990).

John Milbank, *Theology and Social Theory: Beyond Secular Reason*, 2nd ed. (Oxford, UK: Blackwell, 2006).

H. Richard Niebuhr, *Christ and Culture* (New York: Harper & Row, 1951).

Ron Sider, *The Scandal of the Evangelical Conscience: Why Are Christians Living Just Like the Rest of the World?* (Grand Rapids, MI: Baker Books, 2005).

Christian Smith, *American Evangelicalism: Embattled and Thriving* (Chicago: University of Chicago Press, 1998).

On the social strategies of Christian churches, see

Dorothy Day, *The Long Loneliness: The Autobiography of Dorothy Day* (New York: Harper, 1952).

Stanley Hauerwas and William H. Willimon, *Resident Aliens: Life in the Christian Colony* (Nashville: Abingdon Press, 1989).

Tim LaHaye, *Left Behind: A Novel of the Earth's Last Days* (Wheaton, IL: Tyndale House Publishers, 1995).

George A. Lindbeck, *The Nature of Doctrine: Religion and Theology in a Postliberal Age* (Philadelphia: Westminster Press, 1984).

H. Richard Niebuhr, *The Social Sources of Denominationalism* (New York: Henry Holt, 1929), a classic in this field.

Rousas John Rushdoony, *The Institutes of Biblical Law* (Nutley, NJ: Craig Press, 1973).

Ernst Troeltsch, *The Social Teaching of the Christian Churches* (Louisville, KY: Westminster John Knox Press, 1992).

Jim Wallis, *God's Politics: Why the Right Gets It Wrong and the Left Doesn't Get It* (San Francisco: HarperOne, 2005).

PART V

Part V's historical perspective presents numerous themes, each of which is the subject of many complex and worthy volumes of historical research. Here are some of those volumes.

David Bebbington, *Evangelicalism in Modern Britain: A History from the 1730s to the 1980s* (London: Unwin Hyman, 1989).

Gary J. Dorrien, *The Making of American Liberal Theology: Imagining Progressive Religion, 1885–1900* (Louisville, KY: Westminster John Knox Press, 2003).

———, *The Making of American Liberal Theology: Idealism, Realism, and Modernity, 1900–1950* (Louisville, KY: Westminster John Knox Press, 2003).

———, *The Remaking of Evangelical Theology* (Louisville, KY: Westminster John Knox Press, 1998).

William R. Hutchison, *The Modernist Impulse in American Protestantism* (Durham, NC: Duke University Press, 1992).

George M. Marsden, *Fundamentalism and American Culture* (New York: Oxford University Press, 1980).

———, *Understanding Fundamentalism and Evangelicalism* (Grand Rapids, MI: Eerdmans Publishing Company, 1991).

Mark A. Noll, *The Rise of Evangelicalism: The Age of Edwards, Whitefield, and the Wesleys* (Downers Grove, IL: Intervarsity Press, 2004).

Robert Wuthnow, *The Restructuring of American Religion* (Princeton, NJ: Princeton University Press, 1988).

———, *The Struggle for America's Soul: Evangelicals, Liberals, and Secularism* (Grand Rapids, MI: Eerdmans Publishing Company, 1989).

Index